Who Dares Wins Publishing
www.whodareswinspublishing.com
445 Ridge Springs Drive
Chapel Hill, NC 27516

Copyright © 2012 Victoria Martínez
All rights reserved

Without limiting the rights under copyright reserved above, no part of this publication may be re-produced, stored in or introduced into a retrieval system, or transmitted, in any form or by any means (electronic, mechanical, photocopying, recording or otherwise), without the prior written permission of the copyright owner of this book.

TABLE OF CONTENTS

An Unusual Journey through Royal History Volume I   5
  Dedication   7
  Foreword   1
  Praise for Victoria Martínez   3
  More Praise   4
  Acknowledgements   6
  Introduction   9
  An "Illustrated" Royal History   11
  The Monarchy, Sewers and Modernization   16
  The Thin Blue Bloodline   21
  Royalty: From Reverence to Obsession   26
  Worthy of *Our* Custom   31
  Is He or Isn't He?   36
  Royal Acts of Admonition   42
  Reigning at Sea: Beyond Ruling the Waves   47
  The Pudding King and Other Royal Christmas Trivia   52
  Little People at Royal Courts   55
  The Real and Surreal Royals   63
  The King's Evil   67
  The Offbeat Legacy of Royal Eponyms   72
  Chiefly Royal Relations   75
  Queen of Where Else?   79
  A Pageant of Queens   84
  The Courting of Fat Mary   93
  Bugger Bognor… How's the Empire?   106

An Unusual Journey through Royal History Volume II   112
  Dedication   114
  Foreword   116
  Praise for Victoria Martínez   118
  More Praise   120
  Acknowledgements   122
  Introduction   124
  The Larger-Than-Life Württembergs   126

Secondhand Queens	133
When Queens Trump	141
Royalty for a Day	150
Princess Margaret: Neither Love Nor Money	155
The Crown of Saint Wenceslas	160
Shaping Princes and States	160
Good King Wenceslas	162
A Kingdom Emerges	163
The Czech Golden Age	165
Chaos	167
Disappearing Into History	168
Almost a Queen	171
The Monarchy Giveth, Taketh and, Sometimes, Disposeth	177
Happy Princesses of Wales: A Royal Oxymoron	182
The Empress Who Longed to be a Queen	192
Princess Ka'iulani: Princess of the Peacocks	197
Born to Rule, Like it or Not	201
The Royal Nunnery	207
Queen Kleptomaniac?	217
More Books by Victoria Martínez	222
Author Bio	224

An Unusual Journey through Royal History
Volume I
by

Victoria Martínez

DEDICATION

To my dear friend, Amy Cohen, who told me so.

Foreword

Royalty – so many people think of it as an anachronistic and even atavistic institution that has absolutely no relevance to today's complex world.

Indeed... who cares about these obscure sepia photographs, people stiffly looking into the camera in uniforms and tiaras, frowning, and sometimes glassy-eyed? Who cares about these pretentious people who seemed to be fiddling while Rome burned, or eating cake while Paris raged?

Surely these frizzy haired women and mustachioed men are only of interest to hobbyists – people fascinated with obscure genealogies, jewelry, those selfsame photographs, collectables and ceremonial intricacies.

The truth is that royalty has more relevance than what is readily apparent on the surface. They aren't just celebrities, or scandals. They are much, much more. Celebrities are usually only of interest because of how they dress, where they go and with whom they are associated either professionally or romantically. Being a true royal is about country, duty, family and setting an example of service and devotion to the people. While not all Royals have embraced these sterling attributes, these are at least the qualities that, in my opinion, define and set aside the Queen of Spain from, say, a famous actor or pole-vaulter.

However, reading these articles should also gives a sense that they are human beings who put on their shoes one foot at a time, like everyone else. Possibly, one of the biggest differences between them and us is that they know their genealogies for hundreds of years in the past.

And why? Probably because some unusually energetic and obscure ancestor in the 9th or 12th or 11th century coerced or bribed or charmed the locals to help him take the next hill. Thereafter they celebrated this hardy soul (and his family after him) as he became the Count, the Duke, or the Marquis of such and such, and the rulers of so and so.

Reading these different articles should give insight not only to the subjects they encapsulate, but also a personification of the society in which they dwell. In each personality is a reflection of their times, culture or lack thereof, the events and their various families.

Thus getting back to my main point, and that is the relevance of such reading. Looking at subjects such as: marriage, circumcision, smoking or even tattoos really tells us just how human these subjects really are, and how their seemingly larger lives are merely a reflection of our own.

Ilana D. Miller

Ilana D. Miller is an Adjunct Professor of History at Pepperdine University in Malibu and the Senior Editor of the *European Royal History Journal*. Her publication credits include the non-fiction narrative *Reports from America: William Howard Russell and the Civil War* (Sutton Publishing: 2001), several scholarly articles in Historical magazines, as well as historical fiction.

An Unusual Journey Through Royal History

Praise for Victoria Martínez

If there's one thing I know about Tori Martínez after seven years of friendship, it's that she loves to travel. Intellectually and physically, Tori is always at large in the world, gathering information and then putting it down on paper in a style which is alive with the pleasure of translating her themes into words.

As you'll know if you're buying this book, Tori's great love is history. Whether it be the story of women's experiences or the history of royal houses, she brings the same light touch to all.

Who can resist an opening line like this:

"It may be slightly surprising to see the words 'monarchy' and 'sewer' appear together in the same sentence, but the two have actually shared a very close connection for quite some time."?

Toilets, tattoos, obsessive fans and bickering relations: Tori highlights the most entertaining side of royal history, but her knowledge is phenomenal and essentially scholarly.

What more can I say? This a lovely, entertaining collection of articles she has written, and it is wonderful to see Tori in print again after a very difficult period in her life which has handled with grace and humour, and with the ever-present support of her husband David.

Janet Ashton, author of "The German Woman" and co-author of "The Grand Dukes"

Victoria Martínez

More Praise

"I enjoyed these essays on royalty, which range widely from the beauty of Queens to court dwarfs and royal circumcision. Readers will find an impressively wide span of history enjoyably investigated." – Hugo Vickers

Hugo Vickers, author of "Behind Closed Doors: The Tragic, Untold Story of The Duchess of Windsor," is a writer and broadcaster who has written biographies of many twentieth century figures.

"*An Unusual Journey Through Royal History* is exactly what its title suggests. It is a compilation of historical royal trivia: noteworthy, perhaps, definitely rare and, at times, inconceivable. It certainly makes the study of royal history an interesting quagmire, a Pandora's Box, of the strange, the unusual and, perhaps, sometimes the sordid anomalies of very public lives.

"Martinez writes in an inviting style, with interesting descriptions and commentary, coupled with lots of well-researched historical facts. *An Unusual Journey Through Royal History* is a fascinating collection of royal trivia, well written, well researched and well presented. Well done!"

An Unusual Journey Through Royal History

An Unusual Journey Through Royal History is highly recommended by award-winning author and Allbooks reviewer, Emily-Jane Hills Orford, Allbooks Review International (www.allbooksreviewint.com).

ACKNOWLEDGEMENTS

As a child, I was surrounded by history. Growing up in New Jersey, my parents always made sure I knew the historical significance of where we lived. Almost every weekend or vacation, we traveled all over the country, almost always to somewhere historically important. At each place we stayed – old inns, plantations, farms, houses and even a former brothel or two – I would imagine myself as an original resident and try to grasp what life was like "back then."

When we weren't going somewhere historical, my parents told me stories about our family's history and taught me to use my imagination to travel back in time. This is a technique I perfected when I took to calling myself "Queen Victoria", sat in my pink velvet throne with a faux fur rug draped over my shoulders and adorned with my grandmother's paste jewelry, my sister at my feet swearing fealty. It wasn't long before I graduated to books that most children wouldn't touch even under threat of torture, soon finding my niche of obscure, misunderstood or overlooked elements of history.

Now, I think of my love of history as a seed that grew and flourished in the fertile soil of my childhood with my parents, Jim and Grace Van Orden, as the chief gardeners. Without them, I wouldn't be pursuing my passion today. I also would never have had my first audience – one that is now my longest and, sometimes, most critical.

Despite my love of history, I also have a practical side. I knew that I wanted to write, but I also knew that I didn't want to be a starving writer, so I entered the corporate world with two degrees in communications as a public relations professional and made a living writing for – and sometimes as - other people. My historical writing was a mere sideline until I decided to take a chance by quitting my job, selling all my belongings, and moving to England to research and write.

Little did I know that by looking into the past I would find my own future: my husband, David Martínez Ortega. A Spaniard also living in London, he won my heart by giving me the best gift a potential love-interest ever gave me: a book about history. He believed in me and my writing from the start, and it was while we were still dating that I had my first chance to widely publish my personal writing in a weekly column for the Unofficial Royalty website (http://www.unofficialroyalty.com). David even helped me come up with my pen name for the column: The Royal Scribe.

The owner of Unofficial Royalty, Geraldine Voost (now a good friend), liked my sample article enough to give me a weekly column on her very popular website. I wrote many articles for two wonderful years, and all but one of the articles in this book originally appeared on her site.

The only article in this book that did not appear on the Unofficial Royalty website was published in two beautiful journals: *The European Royal History Journal*, published in the United States by Arturo Beéche; and *Royalty Digest Quarterly*, published in Sweden by Ted Rosvall. Both publications have been wonderful forums for my writing over the last few years.

Of course, I have to thank all my friends who have always read whatever I've written, as well as my mentors and friends,

Ilana Miller and Janet Ashton, for guiding and encouraging me through all the ups and downs of the writing life.

Last, but certainly not least, I owe special thanks to Jen Talty and Bob Mayer at Who Dares Wins Publishing for seeing something special in my writing and for publishing what I hope will be the first of many books with them.

An Unusual Journey Through Royal History

INTRODUCTION

This is not your typical royal history book.

The stories here don't belong in either textbooks or tabloids. Everything is true and well-documented, but not scholarly or pedantic. Some of the topics are silly, while others are serious. Each article touches on an overlooked or unusual aspect of royal history, spanning centuries and countries, but in no particular order.

From first to last, they will take you on a journey through royal history you've probably never seen or thought of before. As a writer and historian, I enjoy taking this kind of ride through history, and I like taking people along with me to demonstrate that history doesn't have to be boring or sensationalized to be interesting.

All but one of the articles in this book were originally published online at the Unofficial Royalty website, where I was a regular contributor for two years. One, "The Courting of Fat Mary," was published in two respected royal history journals: *The European Royal History Journal* and *Royalty Digest Quarterly*. They've been edited and updated for this volume and selectively compiled from many articles I've written over the years to take you on this unusual royal journey.

We live in a modern world where the institution of royalty both puzzles and fascinates us. Kings, queens, emperors and dynasties dominate almost any world history, while more modern monarchs, heirs and wayward royals still rule the headlines. In an age where we know monarchs are not God's representatives on Earth, we still seek to canonize, lionize and demonize them. But the bottom line is, they are - and always have been - mere humans, with histories and stories that we can laugh at, relate to and identify with.

I hope you enjoy this unusual journey through royal history as much as I enjoyed writing it.

An "Illustrated" Royal History

The last Anglo-Saxon king of England lay dead on a battlefield near Hastings, an arrow through his eye. William the Bastard of Normandy was now William the Conqueror of England.

William's next, most immediate problem was to positively confirm that the corpse before him did indeed belong to his vanquished rival, Harold II – a task made difficult by the dead man's disfigured face. The solution came in the shape of Edith Swan Neck, King Harold's longtime mistress, who identified her dead lover by the words "Edith and England" tattooed on his chest, just one of several such illustrations on his body.

While not all stories of royal tattoos are quite so dramatic, just the concept of "royal tattoos" can seem incongruous to our modern perceptions of royalty. After all, it was only in the late 1990s that Zara Philips, daughter of Britain's Princess Anne, caused a media sensation simply for having her tongue pierced. Relatively speaking, it should probably come as a far greater surprise that the supposedly prim and proper Victorian era was high season for tattooing among royalty and the aristocracy.

King Edward VII helped pioneer the fashion in Britain when, as Prince of Wales, he had a Jerusalem Cross tattooed on his arm during a visit to Jerusalem in 1862. Twenty years later, his sons – Prince Eddy, the ill-fated heir to the throne, and Prince George, the future George V – both had dragons tattooed on their arms during a visit to Japan. Before returning home, they stopped in Jerusalem to be further illustrated by the same artist who had tattooed their father.

Queen Victoria may or may not have been amused upon learning about her grandsons' new body art, but their mother, Alexandra, Princess of Wales, reportedly was most certainly not amused when she was told incorrectly that the tattoos were on their faces, not their arms. Despite her undoubted horror at imagining the tattooed faces of her sons, Alexandra probably had nothing against more discreet tattoos, even among the women of her set.

Lady Randolph Spencer Churchill (*née* Jennie Jerome), the American heiress, society beauty, and mother of Winston Churchill, circulated quite freely among the Wales' social circle sporting a tattoo of a snake around her left wrist. A well-placed bracelet hid the tattoo when it didn't tickle her fancy. Her son Winston followed suit and had an anchor tattooed on his forearm, *à la* Popeye. Even Alexandra's sister-in-law, Queen Olga of Greece (1851-1926) – Prince Philip, Duke of Edinburgh's paternal grandmother – reportedly had a tattoo.

Still more royals outside Britain were getting "inked" around the same time. Another of Queen Victoria's grandsons, Kaiser Wilhelm II of Germany, had a tattoo, as did George V's cousin, Czar Nicholas II of Russia. Actually, royal tattoos were common in Russia long before Britain caught on – it seems Peter the Great (1689-1725) and Catherine the Great (1729-1796) both had tattoos.

Immediately following the Victorian era, royalty continued to be tattooed at a fairly rapid rate. Austrian Archduke Franz Ferdinand, whose assassination in 1914 sparked World War I, had a "lucky" snake tattooed on his right hip – reportedly the exact place where the deadly bullet hit him. In Spain, King Alfonso XIII and his son, the Count of Barcelona (grandfather and father of the present king of Spain, respectively), both had tattoos.

One of the most heavily tattooed royals of the modern era was King Frederik IX of

Denmark (1899-1972), whose body art included a Chinese dragon on his chest, various anchors and even the family crest elsewhere on his body. His grandson and our contemporary, Crown Prince Frederik of Denmark, has followed the tradition with at least two tattoos of his own – a shark from his Danish navy days and a Nordic symbol.

Other modern royals with tattoos include Princess Stephanie of Monaco, with at least six that are visible, and Juliana Guillermo, the daughter of Princess Christina of the Netherlands, who bears a small one on her ankle. Back to Britain, Zara Philips is also rumored to have a tattoo. There is even speculation that the current Prince of Wales has a tattoo. Whether the sources are simply misunderstanding the frequent connection of Charles' name with the British term "military tattoo" – which is, in fact, a military parade – or are possibly confusing him with his great-great grandfather is open to question. Perhaps most interesting of all the theories is that Queen Victoria herself may have had an "intimately placed" tattoo.

While the appearance of tattoos on royalty may have sparked greater social acceptance of the practice, the real credit for the trend actually belonged to two explorers – William Dampier and Captain James Cook. On his return to London in 1691, Dampier brought with him a heavily tattooed South Sea Islander who was introduced at the court of King William III and

Queen Mary II and would become known as "Giolo, the Famous Painted Prince." Famous, perhaps, but it was Omai, the tattooed Polynesian warrior Captain Cook brought to London and presented to King George III in 1774, who really helped start the trend among fashionable society. Cook's voyages also helped perpetuate the idea of tattooed sailors, as many of his crewmen returned home with tattoos of their own.

On a broader level, the overall popularity of tattoos in Britain and around Europe was really just one of the high points in the vastly fluctuating history of tattoos, which dates back to at least the Neolithic period (8500 to 4000 B.C.). The ancient Egyptians are known to have used the art of tattooing for ritualistic practices – on women in particular – as early as 2000 B.C. By 1000 B.C., tattooing had spread to Japan, India, China and the Pacific Islands. Tattooing in Japan was first used to ward off evil spirits, although by 300 A.D. it had become the mark of criminals. Ancient Greek spies used tattoos to communicate their rank and status to one another, while the Romans tattooed criminals and slaves.

Pretty much every part of the known world was tattooing by the time of Christ. Despite a passage in the Bible expressly forbidding tattoos – Leviticus 19:28 reads: "Ye shall not make any cuttings in your flesh for the dead, nor print or tattoo any marks upon you..." – early Christians still tattooed small crosses on their arms to mark their faith. In 787, Pope Hadrian banned tattooing, but the practice continued nonetheless. In particular, the Danes, Norse and Saxons regularly tattooed themselves with family symbols and crests, and the early Britons used tattoos for ceremonial purposes.

This brings us back to poor Harold II, lying dead on that battlefield in 1066, his mistress and his kingdom tattooed on his chest, and William the Conqueror wondering how to identify the body. But while a tattoo may have helped verify William's victory, it seems the Normans didn't like tattoos and the practice largely died along with Harold – that is, until exploration and the Victorian Age once again illustrated royal history.

THE MONARCHY, SEWERS AND MODERNIZATION

It may be slightly surprising to see the words "monarchy" and "sewer" appear together in the same sentence, but the two have actually shared a very close connection for quite some time. This is due largely, but not entirely, to the historically close proximity of the strongholds of the British monarchy to the River Thames, which, up until about 140 years ago, was London's biggest sewer. More tangentially, both the British monarchy and London's sewers owe their current form to the Victorian Era and both have, for some time, been in need of modernization.

The reign of Queen Victoria presided over not only a period of major industrial development, technological advancement and enlightened thinking, but also of major improvements and modernization to the monarchy. By the time of the Great Stink in 1858, when the smell from rotting sewage in the Thames was so bad that Parliament had to be abandoned, the monarchy had evolved from a rather disrespected, if not entirely dissolute, institution to a progressive and meaningful symbol of government and family values.

As the monarchy advanced into a more modern institution, a forward-thinking man named Joseph Bazalgette was tasked with doing the same for London's foul and deadly sewage system – creating an incredibly modern and revolutionary design that transformed the Thames from a cesspit into a free-flowing river and London from a deathtrap to a modern European city.

But, once again, the fates of both the monarchy and the sewers are intertwined. Somehow, once both the monarchy and the sewers were updated to sufficiently accommodate the modern era, they just stopped growing. Sewers that were built to accommodate 2,000,000 people are now expected to serve around 8,000,000, and a monarchy that was well-suited for the Victorian mentality has continued on in much the same way ever since.

Today, we find the British royal family and the sewers of London in much the same place as they were during the Great Stink – catching up with a modern world that has surpassed them in many ways. In both cases, the masses have recognized the need for modernization long before the individuals handling the institutions. For Britain's royal family, the need to grasp onto tradition has generally been the reason that calls for modernization have been eschewed, if not ignored. Ironically, instead of following Queen Victoria's example of modernizing the monarchy, her descendents have been reluctant to change her traditions, most of which are entirely outmoded.

Unfortunately, it usually takes a traumatic event to move a giant machine into action. Several years ago, as pouring rain pushed London's antiquated Victorian sewers to the brink, forcing raw sewage to once again flood into the Thames and creating a modern day Great Stink, there developed a turning point reminiscent of the flood of criticism faced by the British royal family after Diana's death. After years of urging to the monarchy to modernize, the delayed and distant reaction by the royal family was the last straw for most people – things had to change *now*.

Slowly, slowly, they've gotten the idea. Little changes here and there have started to add up into bigger shifts. More topics, it seems, are open to discussion. Less is intentionally hidden from public view. The royal family is starting to be held to more "human" standards – both in terms of fallibility and responsibility. Expectations are both higher and lower. And, as is to be expected, much of the change is coming from the younger generation, with slightly more resistance from the older.

For one thing, the head of the British royal family is an octogenarian, so it's no surprise that the monarchy is often perceived as "out-of-date." You can't expect a woman of her age and trained to a certain standard to be progressively modern. That said, even The Queen is consistently taking actions to update the monarchy – mainly by changing her own outward behavior and responses to the world around her.

While some of the changes may seem trivial or long overdue – like finally changing the rule that in order to avoid turning their back to The Queen, officials must walk backward in her presence at State occasions – others are more profound. First came the open acceptance of controversial figures like Camilla Parker-Bowles and her subsequent marriage to The Prince of Wales. Then Prince William was openly living with Catherine Middleton prior to their marriage, something that just wouldn't have been acceptable a generation ago.

On the other hand, the British monarchy consistently fails the test of modernity when compared to many of the Continental monarchies. Whereas Norway, Sweden and Monaco, among others, were pioneers in changing the laws of succession that once gave male heirs precedence over females, Britain has been among the last to do so. (At the time this book was originally published in April 2011, the laws of succession in Britain still favored males. Britain finally changed the law in October 2011. And while the heirs to the thrones of other European monarchies are marrying who and when they want, archaic marital restrictions are only now beginning to be lifted from senior members of the British royal family.

For our part, we demand change and variety on the one hand and urge tradition and uniformity on the other. And we're both fascinated and horrified with the changes that have been made. Although we profess to desire a more modern, down-to-earth monarchy, we're appalled to learn just how like us members of the royal family can be. We don't seem to want to know that our Tupperware is newer than The Queen's, or that the royals also have leftovers night at the palace. And most of us shudder at the idea of ridding the monarchy of the pomp and pageantry that routinely works us up into a collective frenzy. Modernization is fine, but don't take away our amusements.

Clearly, there's a fine line, and it's not an easy one for an institution as old and big as the monarchy to navigate with ease and speed. We don't always make it easy on them, either. Returning to the sewer analogy, we have to remember that we get what we give. It's the whole 'garbage in, garbage out' mentality. If we expect the royals to be perfect, they will always be doomed to failure and we will always be disappointed. If we challenge them to change, but don't like it when they do, what incentive will they have to keep trying? And if we ask them to modernize, but get impatient with the necessary growing pains, how progressive are *we*?

The bottom line is this – Britain's monarchy, like London's sewers, may be slightly behind the times in many ways, but the foundation is good. With continued attention to the needs of a modern world – and a little more patience from us – the British monarchy can successfully modernize and leave the sewers exclusively to the Victorian Era.

THE THIN BLUE BLOODLINE

For centuries, European royalty validated their regal identity by noting their descent from Charlemagne, the first Holy Roman Emperor. Like their Greek and Roman predecessors, royalty and nobles with Carolingian blood coursing through their veins tended to marry their close or distant relatives in an effort to keep the bloodline relatively pure.

The fact that many of these consanguineous marriages were within the prohibited degrees of common ancestry, according to the Roman Catholic Church, did little to prevent them, especially since the Church was confused over what was considered unacceptable. This was due in part to the fact that the method of calculating consanguinity could not be agreed upon. Acceptable degrees fluctuated between one and seven during the Middle Ages before finally resting at four degrees in 1215. Without getting too much into the details of this extremely confusing area of Canon Law, let's just say that, without a special dispensation from the Church, you weren't supposed to marry your cousins.

Of course, royalty is royalty, and most of the time, they did exactly what they wanted to do, dispensation or no. By the time of William the Conqueror – who was married to his fourth cousin – it is safe to say that the ruling classes in Europe were all pretty much related in some degree. Life carried on in much the same way for William's descendants in England, with the exception that they began using the Canon Laws on consanguinity to their own advantage.

King John is a fine example. As the fifth son of Henry II and Eleanor of Aquitaine, he was better known in his early years as "Lackland". To amend this lack of property, he married Isabella of Gloucester, the daughter and heiress of the Earl of Gloucester, knowing full well that the marriage was contracted within the forbidden degrees of consanguinity (they shared Henry I as a great grandfather). Conveniently, when Isabella produced no children, John had the marriage annulled on – you guessed it – the grounds of consanguinity.

While what John did was characteristically slimy, it was not unusual. He was, in fact, taking from the book of his own mother, who had her marriage to Louis VII of France annulled when she "discovered" that she and her husband were fourth cousins. Once free, Eleanor promptly married the future Henry II of England.

The prevalence of consanguinity among royalty did not necessarily mean that it was thoroughly approved of, especially when politics made outright disgust of it entirely advantageous. This was the case with Richard III, who, it was rumored, wished to dispose of his wife, Anne Neville, in favor of his young niece, Elizabeth of York. Already losing trust and confidence in their king, this was just the excuse Richard's courtiers and enemies needed to incite his final demise. Fortunately for her, Elizabeth escaped marriage to Richard and instead married Henry VII. It was their son who would usher in the next stage of royal marriages.

When the majority of Europe was a part of the Roman Catholic Church, the playing field for royal marriages was fairly wide. A French king could marry an English princess just as easily as an English king could marry a Spanish princess. As long as they were noble and Catholic and, preferably, brought either land or peace with their dowry, one princess was just as good as another. Things got a bit more complicated, however, when Henry VIII of England decided it was in his best interest to break with Rome.

As the matter of religion had become more important – and more controversial – than all other considerations, the pool of prospective royal partners suddenly dwindled. History might have turned out differently if Queen Mary I of England had produced a child with Philip II of Spain (her first cousin once removed), but fate left England leaning towards Protestantism until the Act of Settlement in 1701 officially barred Catholics from the British throne.

Specifically, the Act of Settlement states that only the Protestant descendants of Sophia, Electress of Hanover, who have not married a Catholic, can succeed to the crown. When George I acceded the throne in 1714 under the terms of the Act, he kicked off more than 125 years of intermarriage between his descendants and the many small German principalities. As such, marriage between first cousins was not uncommon – the two most notable instances being the marriage of the future George IV to Caroline of Brunswick, and – of course – Queen Victoria to Prince Albert.

These days, instead of claiming descent from Charlemagne – especially as almost anyone of European descent can make such a claim, myself included – the royalty of Europe now attribute their level of blue-bloodedness to their descent from Queen Victoria. After all, she wasn't known as the "Grandmother of Europe" for nothing. But despite her prolific marriage to Albert, Queen Victoria was a staunch advocate of marriage outside the family, saying, "If there were no fresh blood, the royal race would degenerate morally and physically." Nevertheless, individual members of the British royal family continued to marry their cousins without hesitation. When the future George V's ambitions to marry his first cousin, Princess Marie of Edinburgh, were thwarted, he instead married Princess May of Teck, his second cousin once removed.

With three consanguineous marriages of monarchs in only five generations, it could be said that the royal blood was running a bit thin in Britain. But Queen Victoria would have been proud when her great grandson, Prince Albert, the Duke of York, married Elizabeth Bowes-Lyon in 1923, effectively giving the royal family an infusion of new and hearty Scottish blood. When their daughter fell in love, however, she followed the family pattern, marrying her cousin Prince Philip of Greece. Depending on how you look at it, The Queen and Prince Philip are as distantly related as fourth cousins through their descent from George III, or as closely related as second cousins once removed through King Christian IX of Denmark.

All of this has led us to one place – the line of succession to the British throne. Although the first 67 individuals on the list are British, the majority of the rest of the list is a litany of the foreign descendants of Queen Victoria. Among the first 150 individuals in the line of succession to the British throne today are King Harald V of Norway (68th) and his descendents, as well as many of the remaining members of the royal families of Romania, Yugoslavia, Russia, Prussia, and the various German principalities.

The Norwegians can credit their place in line to Queen Maud of Norway, who was the daughter of Britain's King Edward VII and Queen Alexandra. The Yugoslavian royals owe their position to George V's lost love, Princess Marie of Edinburgh, who became Queen of Romania through her marriage to King Ferdinand of Romania. Marie's sister, Princess Victoria Melita – who became a grand duchess of Russia on her marriage to her first cousin Grand Duke Kyril of Russia – was the progenitor of both the Russian and Prussian royals who now claim a place in the British succession.

Even Queen Elizabeth's own husband is on the list. Prince Philip usually hovers in the range of around 500 or so in line to the throne. Not that this is a strange phenomenon, given that so many monarchs have married near cousins. Queen Mary, for instance, was also in line to the throne independently of her husband, George V.

In short, the heritage and history of the modern British royal family is a tangled and confusing web of marriages and inter-marriages made only slightly less so by the fact that so many royal couples have shared large portions of their respective family trees. It just goes to show that while the royal family has proven that blood is thicker than water in the proverbial sense, the same has not always been true in literal terms.

Royalty: From Reverence to Obsession

The late Diana, Princess of Wales, is often considered incomparable for her combination of charm and seemingly unending charity. Undoubtedly, there's something of a cult of personality about her even after her death. But I'm often asked to liken the obsession with the late Diana, Princess of Wales to any other royals in history.

To begin with, there is no question that Diana was a striking woman with a magnetic personality; a combination of qualities that few individuals really possess, whether they're royals, celebrities or just everyday people. This "certain something" can make all the difference in whether an individual is simply admired or truly adored. Take the Countess of Wessex, for example. She's an attractive, stylish woman whose appearance has even been likened to Diana. Since giving up her professional career, she has spent an increasing amount of time working with charities, even taking on one of Diana's charities. But no matter how many parallels you draw between the two women, Sophie's just missing Diana's vast appeal.

With this in mind, if we look only at recent history – let's say the last 50 years or so – then there are relatively few people in Diana's class. This in no way minimizes the popularity of other royals over the years. Certainly, Queen Elizabeth II has been enormously popular during parts of her reign, particularly the early years. And there's no denying that The Queen Mother in her lifetime was immensely loved. She and George VI were well-loved in Britain for their displays of strength and courage during World War II. Even George V has been called the most popular British male monarch of the 20th century. But if we're talking in terms of "obsession," I think most people would agree hands down that Diana is the modern royal at the top of that list.

That said, there certainly have been individual royals in the more distant past who have captured the attention of the public as much as Diana, but very few of them have had the advantage of modern accessibility to further their existing popularity. Thanks to the proliferation of media reports and a constant barrage of images, Diana was propelled onto a vast global stage that had not previously existed.

What's important to remember is that, historically, most people only knew what the royals looked like through painted portraits or artist's renderings (if they even had access to them). This helped keep the monarchy depersonalized to some extent for most common folk. However, like Diana, her historical counterparts were adept at using the tools available to them to shape and perpetuate their image.

Henry VIII, although alternatively loved and reviled during his lifetime, was one of the first to really understand how to use portraits to convey his power and importance. But where he was good, his daughter was even better. Elizabeth I was a public relations genius who knew exactly how to inspire the love and command the loyalty of her people.

Just one example of her great skill can be seen in the "Rainbow Portrait" located at Hatfield House in Hertfordshire. Aside from just being a distant imposing figure in a portrait, Elizabeth connects with her people by representing herself as a living symbol of all that is important to her subjects. For starters, her gown is covered in eyes and ears indicating that she is the center of attention. A serpent on her sleeve symbolizes wisdom and she holds in her hand a rainbow, which represents peace. Clearly painted on the canvas is the motto, "*Non Sine Sole Iris,*" which literally means, "No rainbow without the sun," but in the symbolic language of the portrait, where Elizabeth is the sun, it essentially translates into – *no peace without Elizabeth*. This ability to shape her image, combined with that "special something" made her an icon equal to Diana without the benefit of modern media.

A great many royals followed in Elizabeth's footsteps, a few even rivaled her in popularity, but Queen Victoria was the next to use available methods with enough skill to make an impression as lasting as Elizabeth. As the book by John Plunkett accurately suggests, Victoria was indeed the first media monarch. It was during her era that photography and the telegraph were invented and mass media took off in a big way. The comings and goings of the royal family were documented more closely than ever and, thanks to improvements in transportation, disseminated quickly throughout the British Empire and the rest of the world. But the news media was still in its infancy during much of Victoria's reign and the royal machine largely controlled the images and messages that were released to the public.

It wasn't really until Edward VIII, later The Duke of Windsor, was Prince of Wales that this started to change. Cameras went from bulky contraptions requiring much maintenance and set-up to hand-held devices that could go just about anywhere. With illiteracy at an all-time low and popular journalism at its peak, newspapers were hungry for candid photos of the royals to accompany the latest gossip.

As a very active member of the royal family, not to mention a very energetic and sociable individual, the young Prince of Wales was a prime candidate for the photographer's lens and became an extremely popular and recognizable royal. While the world at large had always been familiar with the British royals, it was somewhat at arm's length; but the growing global press and the prince's constant international travels helped make him a worldwide figure, rather than just a British one.

And just as Diana was considered the "people's princess," the Prince of Wales was very much a people's prince. No longer relying on official portraits and the image of the royals they were intended to portray, the public could now see for themselves what the royals were really like and develop their own opinions about their characters. With the Prince of Wales, they saw a relaxed and informal man of the people and decided overwhelmingly that they liked him. He may have been the bane of the royal family's existence and, in the end, the wrong man to be king, but he was deeply loved by the public right up to his abdication.

This brings us back to the last 50 years again and, in particular, to Princess Margaret, who was very nearly an early Diana. As a young woman, Princess Margaret's good looks, style and jet-set ways were a constant fascination with the press and the people. She was the modern ideal of a princess and was always doing something to get the media's attention. But Margaret lacked the true personal magnetism of Diana and, in retrospect, didn't make much of a real connection with the people.

Diana, on the other hand, was a commoner (albeit an aristocrat) who worked in a common job when her engagement to Prince Charles was announced. As a result, people instantly connected with her; a feeling that was only magnified when they saw how much she catered to them. She released audio tapes that one of the ways she handled the rejection she felt from the royal family was to throw herself into interaction with the public and, later, her charities. Like Edward, Prince of Wales before her, she made that vital connection with the people; but she went one step farther and gave the public the love and attention no royal had ever given them before. In return, they devoted themselves to her and expressed their love for her in an intensely personal and loyal way. Of course, this sense of intimacy only increased the impact of her early and tragic death, giving millions of people the impression that they had lost someone close to them.

While our ancestors may have been captivated by other royals and the rise of the mass media has certainly made them more accessible to us, at the end of they day, our obsession with Diana comes down to something as unique as Diana was: our sense that she loved us just as much as we loved her.

An Unusual Journey Through Royal History

WORTHY OF *OUR* CUSTOM

Her Majesty The Queen may not personally discuss her pest control needs with Rokill Limited, Queen Elizabeth The Queen Mother probably never smoked Havana cigars from James J. Fox. And it's highly unlikely that Prince Charles, Prince of Wales picks-up his own dry cleaning from Jeeves of Belgravia. But each gave these particular businesses his or her stamp of approval by granting them a Royal Warrant.

With roots dating back to the Middle Ages, Royal Warrants are essentially seals of approval bestowed by select members of the royal family to individuals or companies that have regularly supplied them with goods or services for at least five consecutive years. There are very few other official requirements to become a Royal Warrant holder, although there are restrictions. First, the warrants are issued only to businesses of trade and not to professions, government departments or "places of refreshment or entertainment," among others. Second, holders of warrants are not permitted to disclose specific details about the goods or services they provide – only a general reference. Finally, if a person or business wants to gain a warrant from Prince Charles in particular, it must first prove that it has a "sustainable environmental policy and action plan."

Currently, only The Queen, her husband, Prince Philip, and The Prince of Wales can grant Royal Warrants, although The Queen Mother also granted them during her lifetime and those companies were allowed to keep their warrants for five years after her death. Once granted a Royal Warrant, the individual or company can add the phrase, "By Appointment to [name and title of whomever made the appointment]," as well as the specified Arms or Badge of that particular royal, to its advertising, packaging, stationery, and even its building and vehicles. The warrant does not imply that the company is the only particular supplier of its kind to that royal, but rather recognition that it is the *preferred* supplier.

Royal patronage has undoubtedly been important to trades people throughout history, but it wasn't until Royal Charters were created that these suppliers were officially awarded with royal recognition. According to The Royal Warrant Holders Association, Henry II granted the earliest recorded Royal Charter in 1155 to the Weavers' Company. In the 15th century, the Royal Charter became the Royal Warrant of Appointment, which continues to this day. Like today, some very recognizable figures were given Royal Warrants, including William Caxton, the first English printer, in 1476. By the end of the 18th century, warrant holders were permitted to display the Royal Arms to advertise their distinguished status. Among the more interesting suppliers to receive warrants throughout history were an "Operator for the Teeth," a "Goffe-club Maker," and a "Bug Taker." Even now, some Royal Warrant holders perhaps seem a bit out of the ordinary to the rest of us. G.B. Kent and Sons, for instance, has been "brush maker" to the royal family since the reign of George III. The company even brags on its web site that it made William IV's toothbrushes. Today, the company, which claims it is best known for its hand-made hairbrushes, holds The Queen's Royal Warrant. Price's Patent Candle may be a newer warrant holder than Kent, but its products have certainly been more high profile than hair and toothbrushes – even if most of us didn't know it – as they have been supplying candles to the royal family since the 1850s. Most notably, Price's has supplied the candles for all royal state occasions since the Duke of Wellington's funeral in 1852. More recently, the company's candles have melted elegantly at both the wedding of Prince Charles and Lady Diana in 1981 and the funeral of Diana in 1997.

Like Kent and Price's, a number of Royal Warrant holders have held the honor for between 100 and 200 years. Many of these owe their existence to Queen Victoria and her family, who were more enthusiastic Royal Warrant Grantors than any other royals before or since, granting more than 2000 during her 64-year reign. Fortnum and Mason and Schweppes are just two companies that owe their original warrants to the Victorian royals.

Today, there are around 800 Royal Warrant holders, although some of them have more than one Royal Warrant. Ainsworths Homeopathic Pharmacy, for instance, has warrants from both The Queen and Prince Charles. Only a handful of suppliers have a Warrant from all three authorized royals, one being Benney, a London gold and silversmith. The number of Royal Warrants also changes frequently as new warrants are added and others expire.

Of course, what is given can also be taken away. Although all Royal Warrants are granted for renewable five-year periods, they are reviewed regularly and can be cancelled at any time. Although truly at the Grantor's pleasure, the official reasons for canceling a warrant include: a decline in quality or the discontinuation of the product or service; diminished need for a product or service; or the business goes out of business, changes ownership or is declared bankrupt.

Whatever the case, the company is given 12 months to completely eradicate any indication of the warrant from its product and company. In early 1999, supposedly under pressure from Prince Charles, The Queen withdrew a 122-year-old Royal Warrant from Gallaher Limited, makers of Benson & Hedges cigarettes, which had originally been granted by another Prince of Wales, the future King Edward VII. The official reason for the withdrawal of the warrant, according to Buckingham Palace, was that smoking was no longer popular in the royal family, nor was there enough of a demand for tobacco products.

Late in 1999, following Mohamed al-Fayed's claim that Prince Philip masterminded Diana's death, it was announced that Prince Philip was withdrawing his Royal Warrant of Harrods. Apparently unfazed, al-Fayed promptly proceeded to have not only Prince Philip's name and Royal Seal removed from anything related to Harrods, he also removed everything related to the Royal Warrants of The Queen, The Queen Mother, and Prince Charles, despite the fact that those warrants had not yet expired or been withdrawn.

Controversy has also been raised in regard to the benefits that may be received by the royals who grant the warrants. Although organizations like the Royal Warrant Holders Association insist that Royal Warrants neither cost the warrant holder anything nor provide the Grantor with any free products or services, the exact opposite was contended in late 2002 when Prince Charles' "lavish" lifestyle received massive press coverage. The Prince was accused of bestowing Royal Warrants to obtain free and discounted products for himself, his family and certain members of his staff. *The Observer* even claimed that, among other things, the Prince received free toothpaste from

GlaxoSmithKline in return for granting the company a Royal Warrant.

But regardless of whether or not the royal family benefits from the Royal Warrant system, one thing is clear, it certainly couldn't hurt an individual or business to have the royal seal of approval. Although, as honors go, Royal Warrants are more symbolic than anything, it doesn't take a whole lot of figuring to realize that most people will automatically assume that if it's good enough for royalty, it must be the best.

In The Queen's speech to the Royal Warrant Holder's Association in 2002, she stated that the "Royal Warrant of Appointment is an ancient and honourable institution" and warrant holders are "setting standards in terms of quality and performance which others are obliged to note if not to emulate." Just the school of thought someone like Hyacinth Bucket from the classic BBC comedy series, "Keeping up Appearances," would pursue with a comical vengeance.

Is He or Isn't He?

This is not a subject for everyone – especially the faint of heart or mind. Nearly everything about the subject at hand is controversial, and mention of it is virtually guaranteed to garner strong emotion among everyone from scholars and medical professionals to parents and their children. But, as with other hotly debated topics, most people find themselves inexorably drawn to knowing more about it, particularly when it concerns the most famous and important. So, as an avowed impartial observer, I write about male circumcision not to polemicize, but rather to explore its place at the heart of modern and recently historical European monarchies.

At first glance, it may seem a bit strange to some people to even connect European monarchies to a practice that is so readily and directly associated with Judaism, given that the two are almost always mutually exclusive. The truth of the matter is, religion has both everything and nothing to do with circumcision among the European royal families. If anything – at least where royalty is concerned – circumcision frequently has a direct connection to dynasty. For starters, think King Louis XVI of France and Czar Peter III of Russia. Popular history tells us that both monarchs suffered from a medical condition called phimosis, which required circumcision in order to allow them to consummate their respective marriages and produce heirs to their thrones.

In Peter's case, the story goes that as the young heir to the Russian throne, he was unable to consummate his marriage with his equally young German bride, Catherine. For nearly 10 years, the royal couple failed to produce an heir. Finally, in 1754, Catherine became pregnant, presumably by her husband. The problem was, despite her husband's obvious attentions to other women, it was widely believed that he could not perform sexually at all due to phimosis. With Catherine pregnant, reportedly by a lover she was encouraged to take by the Empress Elizabeth, something had to be done to remove Peter's physical obstacle and, accordingly, any doubt that the child was his. Thus, Catherine's lover reportedly got Peter so drunk he either agreed to or couldn't defend himself against circumcision and was subsequently able to consummate the marriage.

As for Louis XVI, it seems he, too, found himself unable to consummate his marriage to his Austrian wife, Marie Antoinette. For three years, it was believed that the problem was a psychological one – a point that seemed to be verified when, in 1773, the then Dauphin proclaimed conjugal victory. It was a short-lived triumph if there ever was one. Sexual relations between the couple were troublesome and unfruitful, and it wasn't until 1777 that Marie Antoinette's brother got to the root of the trouble with Louis and convinced the King to agree to a circumcision for his phimosis. Less than a year later, the Queen was pregnant.

In both cases, it would appear that circumcision not only ensured the future of the monarchy (or so it seemed at the time), but, as a cure to phimosis, it also provided an excellent public excuse as to why both royal couples failed to execute their primary duty in a reasonable amount of time.

The problem is, wherever circumcision is concerned, there is almost always disagreement; and, naturally, the more high-profile the individual, the greater the debate. So as not to forget the other side, it must be said that both Peter's and Louis' circumcisions are contested, with most challenges stating that both arguments were fabricated as either political or religious propaganda by either the royal "machines" to assuage rumors or by various religious factions to bolster their own beliefs or discredit an institution. These arguments also apply to more modern claims of royal circumcision and could at least partially explain why most all modern European monarchies are exceedingly tight-lipped about the subject (aside from the fact that it is a most *personal* subject).

This is certainly the case when you consider the Spanish royal family. Queen "Ena" of Spain, a granddaughter of Queen Victoria, discovered that her son, Prince Alfonso of Spain, was a hemophiliac during his circumcision. Now, as then, circumcision is not terribly common in Spain, which raises many questions about why Ena and her husband, King Alfonso XIII of Spain, chose to circumcise their son and if that tradition continues in the Spanish royal family today. The answer, at least to me, remains elusive; however, there are various theories that can be made based on what information is available.

It is, for instance, widely speculated in Spain that King Juan Carlos is circumcised, as is the custom among males in the Spanish royal family. This information is directly stated in *El Rey (Conversaciones Privadas con Don Juan Carlos I de España)*, a book written by Spanish journalist José Luis de Villalonga who, along with another journalist, had intimate access to and exclusive interviews with the King and his family.

If true (and, from what I understand, it *is* a disputed point), the question remains – how did the tradition begin among the Catholic Spanish royals? Some claim that, as a preponderance of doctors in Medieval Spain were Jewish, circumcision was practiced on royal males as a matter of course. This information I simply paraphrase from other opinions. Personally, given the complicated history of Spanish/Jewish relations during the Middle Ages, I choose to leave any attempts at either validating or disproving this theory to scholars. That said, I personally wonder if the practice of circumcision among the Spanish royals is in anyway related to the fact that the Spanish kings, as successors of the royal family of Naples, hold the title of King of Jerusalem. Even today, King Juan Carlos of Spain bears this ancient title. Once again, however, I leave this question to others far more qualified in that particular area of history.

From where I stand, I lean toward the theory that Queen Ena – born Princess Victoria Eugénie of Battenberg and the youngest granddaughter of Britain's Queen Victoria – introduced circumcision to the Spanish royal family. After all, if she introduced the Christmas tree, golf and horse racing to her adopted country, why not circumcision? In all seriousness, however, it's possible that the tradition, which many people are surprised to learn was introduced into the British royal family by none other than Queen Victoria, was spread to other royal families by her many children and grandchildren. It's purely speculation on my part and I find little evidence to point that other modern monarchies practice circumcision, but there is little doubt that circumcision has been a part of the British royal family ever since Queen Victoria.

An idealistic woman and a romantic at heart, it probably took little encouraging to convince Queen Victoria that she was descended from none other than the Biblical King David. Certainly, it must have been an idea that was not only utterly attractive, but perhaps appealed to her dynastic sensibilities. At a time when royal subjects the world over were daily reasserting – in words and action – the belief that their monarchs were most certainly not chosen by God, it must have been a way of justifying her and her family's elevated status. It wasn't just Victoria, either, who believed in the King David connection. The "British Israel" movement, which stated (among other things) that the British people were descended from one of the Ten Lost Tribes of Israel, was very popular before, during and after Victoria's reign. In accordance with this belief, Victoria – along with much of the British aristocracy – chose to have her sons circumcised. And the tradition has continued, according to most every account, right up to the modern day.

In fact, it's incredibly easy to find various sources that cite the current Prince of Wales' circumcision at Buckingham Palace in 1948 by Rabbi Jacob Snowman, M.D., who was the official Mohel (Jewish ritual circumciser) of the London Jewish community. Interestingly, by most accounts Princes William and Harry were *not* circumcised as infants, reportedly because the Princess of Wales refused to have it done on her young sons, although some sources claim she *did* agree to have it done. The opinion is even more divided on whether or not the *un*circumcised royal princes were requested by their father to have the procedure after their mother's death. It has been rumored that Prince Harry agreed and had the procedure only months after Diana's death, while Prince William refused. Whatever the case, as with most issues regarding the two princes, this is an extremely controversial issue and is unlikely to be affirmatively ascertained one way or another.

With that in mind, I feel it necessary to say that, if you're like I was, and looking for categorical proof that *anyone* royal was or is circumcised, I'm afraid it's a bit like squeezing blood from a turnip (no pun intended). Sure, biographers and journalists will write what they either believe to be true or have heard through the grapevine, but in all reality, it's highly unlikely that any royal ever did or ever will come right out and say, "I am/am not circumcised." It's just not done. And who can blame them? At the end of the day, it is truly a personal matter and, in my opinion, I've found the history surrounding the use and practice of the tradition among royalty and, accordingly, the impact that practice has had on history, far more interesting than whether someone *is* or *isn't*.

Royal Acts of Admonition

As if finding "the one" wasn't difficult enough already for us common folk, Britain's royal legacy has made it even more challenging for those lucky enough to be close to the throne. In the days when most royal marriages were arranged, the royal acts controlling marriage – The Act of Settlement and The Royal Marriages Act – were more of a technicality than the major stumbling block to matrimonial bliss that they are today. Or were they?

Ever since an ambivalent government created it in 1772, The Royal Marriages Act has, at a minimum, proved a bit of a joke, and, at most, left behind a legacy of unwanted and unhappy or broken and bitter royal marriages.

The Act, initiated by the high-minded George III, which prohibited any descendant of George II to marry under the age of 25 without the monarch's permission, was designed to prevent "unsuitable" royal marriages. Unsuitable meaning, naturally, anyone who was not of royal or sufficiently high aristocratic blood, but extending by inference to commoners, bastards, actresses, and all the other vulgar creatures that were increasingly making their way into royal circles.

And while this broad interpretation of "unsuitable" seemed to be in line with a wide variety of possible situations, at the time the king had one particular marriage very much in mind – that of his scandal-prone brother Henry, Duke of

Cumberland, to commoner and widow Anne Horton, who he had secretly wed in 1771. Unfortunately for the king, this unfortunate occurrence was the impetus behind the Act and, therefore, the Act itself was too late to prevent it, but it would certainly keep it from happening again... or so he thought.

In fact, the Act proved ineffectual almost immediately after it was passed. The first blow came when the king's favorite brother, William, Duke of Gloucester, admitted that he, too, had secretly married a widowed commoner, Lady Waldegrave, in 1766. To make matters worse, this new royal duchess was also the illegitimate daughter of Sir Edward Walpole. Once again, since the marriage had taken place before the Act was established, nothing could be done to alter the situation. The king, however, made sure neither duchess was ever received at court, although given the fact that George III's court was considered the dullest in Europe, it would seem they didn't miss very much.

Not only had the Act immediately proved unsuccessful, it had been widely unpopular even before it was passed, not just within the circle of the affected members of the royal family, but with at least two prominent politicians in particular arguing loudly against it. Whig politician Charles James Fox believed that "even" members of the royal family should be able to marry whom they wished, and he resigned his office in retaliation. William Pitt the Elder called the proposed Act "wanton and tyrannical." But, despite these protests, the bill passed into law, thanks largely to the strength of Lord North's Tory government.

As it turned out, it was Charles James Fox, a close friend of George, Prince of Wales, who later strongly urged the Prince not to marry his Catholic mistress, Maria Fitzherbert. In typical fashion, the prince ignored this good advice and in December

1785, he secretly married Maria. Although the Act had again failed to prevent this unsuitable union, the marriage was nonetheless illegal, not only under the Royal Marriages Act, but also under the 1701 Act of Settlement, which prohibits a Catholic or anyone married to a Catholic from ascending the throne (more on this in a minute). In due time, the technical illegality was reinforced by the prince himself who agreed to a "legal" marriage to his first cousin, Caroline of Brunswick, in 1795.

Over the next 150 years, the Royal Marriages Act lay inactive, stirring only to rumor and speculation that this royal or that married someone unsuitable. Among these was Prince Eddy, the Duke of Clarence, who was rumored to have married Annie Crook in the 1880s. Finally, in 1936, the next significant and/or substantiated marriage-related constitutional crisis occurred when Edward VIII decided that Wallis Simpson meant more to him than the crown. So, after a century and a half of nothing but acceptable royal marriages, it's no wonder that The Abdication Crisis made the impact it did.

Then, a mere 19 years later, came Princess Margaret and Group Captain Peter Townsend. In Margaret's case, however, the government made a complete shift in attitude from Edward VIII's proposed marriage to Wallis Simpson. Harkening back to the position of politicians in George III's day, the Lord Chancellor, Lord Kilmuir, was among those who believed that the Royal Marriages Act was outdated and an embarrassment that should be repealed. Reportedly, this sentiment was widespread enough that The Queen was asked if she would agree to its repeal.

This overall sentiment no doubt helped Margaret's case and, combined with various unknown factors, led to the government developing a secret plan that would have allowed her to marry with almost no alteration to her existence (unlike her unfortunate great uncle, the Duke of Windsor). But, as we know, Margaret put duty before love, thus postponing the debate and even the possible repeal of the Royal Marriages Act – a move that may have affected the original marital choice of her nephew, Prince Charles.

More has been said in recent years about repealing the Act of Settlement. Unlike the Royal Marriages Act, which has been actively ignored, widely interpreted, and evaded when necessary, the Act of Settlement has had a more direct affect on those who chose to ignore it. A quick look at the line of succession reveals that at least four people who should be among the first 50 in line to the throne are not, either because they married a Catholic or became one themselves. Interestingly, all of the individuals on the list who have been excluded were unlikely to ever reach the throne anyway due to their relatively low position in the hierarchy.

Created in a time when the British government was more concerned with protecting the monarchy from so-called Papists, the Act of Settlement is today something of a white elephant in our more culturally diverse and tolerant day and age. Or at least that's what we'd like to hope. Personally, as a Protestant married to a Catholic, I am grateful I didn't have to choose between losing my choice of partner or losing my heritage, and it seems a shame to limit the choices of anyone – royalty or not – based on differences in religion.

That said, one argument against the repeal of the Act of Settlement has been that if a Catholic monarch came to the British throne, Church and State would split, as a Catholic monarch cannot be head of the Church of England. Fortunately, at least one aspect of the Act of Settlement has recently been amended. In October 2011, with the change in laws of succession to the throne, the ban on a monarch's (and, presumably, any other member of the royal family) to a marriage to a Catholic has finally been removed.

Clearly, both Acts are important enough to both the future of the monarchy and to our modern sensibilities that they are now being seriously addressed. Along with the changes to the Act of Settlement brought on by the change in succession laws, the British government and Commonwealth countries are also now considering changes to the Royal Marriages Act. Undoubtedly, the outcome will affect the modern and future British royals just as much as they have affected their predecessors. Until then, the cycle continues.

Reigning at Sea: Beyond Ruling the Waves

As glittering as the *RMS Queen Mary 2* is, it just doesn't seem to hold the same appeal as the art deco wonders of the original, grand old *RMS Queen Mary*, which has been permanently docked at the Port of Long Beach in California since 1967. Of course, it also doesn't hurt that the *Queen Mary* is up to her funnels with royal connections, or that she's one of the last real remnants of a dying breed – that of "royal ships."

Once, these royal ships – everything from ferries to warships to ocean liners – numbered too many to count. Their monikers varied from generic references of titles like *Infante*, *Prince of Wales*, *Kaiser*, etc., to specific names like the German *SMS Prinzregent Luitpold* (c. 1913) and the Spanish *Reina Maria Luisa* (c. 1791). Ships were sometimes christened with names that may sound generic today, but were significant at the time. The British merchant vessel *Princess of Denmark* (c. 1687), for instance, was probably named in honor of the marriage of Princess Anne of Britain to Prince George of Denmark in 1683.

Frequently, multiple ships shared the same name or, even more commonly, when an original ship was decommissioned, lost, or damaged beyond repair, the original name was conferred on the replacement ship. This not only explains why certain royals often had several ships named after them (the plethora of Georgian princesses are among the most frequently repeated names), but also why, in modern times, we have the *RMS Queen*

Elizabeth 2 and the *RMS Queen Mary* 2. In fact, it's a common misconception that the *QE2* was named for Britain's Queen Elizabeth II. It was actually named after the first ship of that name, the *RMS Queen Elizabeth*, which was launched in 1938 and named for King George VI's Queen Consort, Queen Elizabeth.

The original *Queen Elizabeth* and *Queen Mary* were sister ships of the Cunard Line and, like sisters, shared a great many experiences. The first "born," the *Queen Mary*, was named after another queen consort, King George V's wife, who christened her in 1934. There is a highly amusing story (discussed in a later chapter) of how Cunard planned to name the ship the *Queen Victoria*, but thanks to a royal misunderstanding between the Line's representative and George V, the ship was named not for the king's grandmother, but for his wife.

While the *Queen Mary* started her life as a luxurious transatlantic ocean liner, breaking speed records along the way, work began on the future *Queen Elizabeth*, which was destined to hold the record as the largest passenger ship ever built until 1996. But her maiden voyage in the Spring of 1940 was under far less glamorous circumstances than her sister ship as she made her way to safety in New York under the cloud of World War II. With the war raging, the Queens – like all other resources in Britain – were needed for the war effort, and both ships were converted and put to work as troop transports, shuttling men and supplies from all over the world. Fortunately, the ships' speed kept them (and millions of troops, wounded soldiers and prisoners of war) safe from the German U-boats throughout the conflict.

After the war, both ships were refitted and returned to luxurious civilian service, playing gracious host to everybody who was somebody – from European royalty to Hollywood stars. One of my favorite nuances of the *Queen Mary* and *Queen Elizabeth* is the idea of the royals as passengers on "their" ships. Not that Queen Elizabeth's voyage on the *Queen Mary* would have garnered anything more than an ironic chuckle, but the Duchess of Windsor likely had to swallow hard when she stepped foot on the ship named after the mother-in-law who scarcely acknowledged her. Sailing on the *Queen Elizabeth* must have been even more difficult for the Duchess given the animosity between the two women, although I somehow think that Wallis managed to ease any personal discomfort by applying her biting sarcasm to the situation at the queen's expense. In any case, the Duchess' fear of flying kept her at sea and, mostly, on the Queens, right up into the 1950s.

By the 1960s, the rising popularity and availability of affordable air travel meant that transatlantic ship voyages were becoming less popular, and in 1969 the Cunard Line replaced both the *Queen Mary* and the *Queen Elizabeth* with the sleeker, faster, and more modern *Queen Elizabeth 2*. The *Queen Mary* was purchased by the City of Long Beach, California and converted into a museum and hotel in the early 1970s. Once again, the *Queen Elizabeth* was less fortunate. In 1970, she was purchased by a Hong Kong shipping magnate who moved the ship to Hong Kong Harbor for conversion to a university. Before the conversion was complete, however, the ship caught fire and attempts to extinguish the fire only served to capsize her. Under the cloud of suspected arson, the *Queen Elizabeth* was finally scrapped in 1975.

Today, the relative handful of "royal ships" is perhaps reflective not only of our need for fast and efficient travel, but also of our increasingly egalitarian society. Fortunately, the legacy of these ships is still there – sometimes in spirit, as in the case of the second generation of Cunard Queens, and sometimes in more tangible form, often as historic attractions. And, like the *Queen Mary* and *Queen Elizabeth*, many of these ships have a history rivaling those of their namesakes.

Some have experienced more than just eventful existences. Like the ship once known as the *Queen Anna Maria*, they've survived any number of incarnations. Originally christened the *Empress of Britain* and launched by Queen Elizabeth II in 1955, the ocean liner was the Canadian Pacific Steamship Company's first following the war. Luxurious as she was, however, she became yet another victim to air travel. Barely 10 years after her first christening, the *Empress of Britain* was sold to the Greek Line to be refitted for New York-to-Mediterranean pleasure cruises. This second incarnation was solemnized when the ship was re-christened the *Queen Anna Maria* and re-launched by her namesake, Queen Anne-Marie of Greece, in 1965.

At the time of the ship's re-christening, the 18-year-old Queen Anne-Marie, a Danish princess by birth, had been Queen of the Hellenes for barely six months; her husband, Constantine II, had been King of the Hellenes for just a year. By 1975, both the King and Queen of the Hellenes and the Greek Line ship *Queen Anna Maria* would be driven out of Greece – the monarchs by political upheaval and the *Queen Anna Maria* by financial troubles. While the King and Queen of the Hellenes went to live in exile, the *Queen Anna Maria* became the *Carnivale* in the Carnival Cruise Line fleet in 1976. She changed hands again in 1993, briefly becoming the *Fiesta Marina* until she was returned to Greek hands in 1995 and renamed the *Olympic*. Finally, she was reincarnated once again, this time into her present form as the charter ship *The Topaz*. I guess it just goes to show that – ship or human – "once a queen" does not mean "always a queen."

On the other hand, the significance of a name often transcends a title. This is certainly the case with what is perhaps one of the most compelling of the early royal ships – the *Mary Rose*. Commissioned by England's Henry VIII in 1509, the ship was named for his beloved sister, Princess Mary, who – as an unwilling pawn in Henry's game of international politics – carried several titles during her life, including Queen of France. Her namesake was used in much the same way, engaging in most of the king's sea battles. Both were also lauded – Mary for her beauty and grace, the *Mary Rose* because as one of the first warships equipped to fire broadside, she was a marvel of her time.

But while Mary died, as the Duchess of Suffolk, quietly in her bed, the fate of the Mary Rose was far from peaceful. Despite an overhaul in 1536, by 1545 she was virtually obsolete and was literally blown over by a strong wind during an altercation with the French fleet, sinking quickly in the Solent Channel near Portsmouth. Initial attempts to raise the *Mary Rose* failed and her location was eventually lost, only to be rediscovered in 1836, and then lost once again. Finally, in 1971, the *Mary Rose* was definitively located and the process of recovery and restoration began in earnest, culminating in the raising of the ship 1982. Today, the *Mary Rose* – along with a great many archaeological finds – is restored and open to visitors in Portsmouth, England.

Like the royals who inspired them, there are simply too many historical royal ships to cover them all, but whether you're a ship enthusiast, royal watcher or both, the legacy of the royal ships will always reign at sea.

The Pudding King and Other Royal Christmas Trivia

The holiday season – a time of year like no other. None can so effectively combine deep religious and spiritual meaning and thoughtful and heartfelt giving with frequently boring and tedious holiday parties and inevitable family bickering. Of course, there's always the fundamental problem of what to talk about during those awkwardly quiet moments. So, whether you're reading this at holiday time or not, I give you this collection of fun and interesting royal Christmas trivia to use to your best advantage to get you through the next holiday season. May you use it to impress your friends and family with your vast knowledge, infuse a boring conversation with something a bit more interesting, halt a more heated family "discussion," or simply melt away into your happy place when the going gets rough.

Most people interested in royalty already know that Queen Charlotte, consort of Britain's King George III, introduced Britain to the German tradition of the Christmas tree, although it was Queen Victoria and Prince Albert who popularized the tradition outside the royal family. But not even that enduring symbol of Christmas would have been possible had it not been for Britain's Charles II.

You see, when the staunchly Puritan Oliver Cromwell took the reins of the British government, he abolished not only the monarchy but also the celebration of Christmas. Although it's wrong to say that he banished Christmas itself, he did ban the objects of merriment that surrounded what he believed should be a strictly pious and religious day. In 1649 – the same year Charles I was executed – Cromwell dictated that Christmas carols, culinary feasts and festive decorations like holly were all forbidden. Those caught celebrating risked arrest. Fortunately, the Merry Monarch restored the celebration of Christmas to a (mostly) grateful nation when he was himself restored to the throne in 1660.

As much as he hated Christmas carols, even Oliver Cromwell would have been pained to argue the good deeds of Wenceslas I, Duke of Bohemia (b. 907) – also known as Saint Wenceslas – who inspired the Christmas carol named for him, "Good King Wenceslas." While the words of the carol tell how the ruler gave alms to a poor peasant on St. Stephen's Day (December 26th, known in Britain as Boxing Day), Wenceslas' is best known for his efforts to promote Christianity in Bohemia and build churches and cathedrals throughout his lands, including the gothic St. Vitus Cathedral in Prague.

While Wenceslas' contribution to Christmas tradition was indirect and spiritual in nature, King George I of Great Britain's contribution was of a more direct and corporeal type. Within months of arriving in London to claim the British throne in 1714, the German whose grasp of the English language was minimal sat down to a Christmas dinner that included a little goody that would become an enduring symbol of an English Christmas – the Christmas pudding. Actually, plum pudding had become the traditional Christmas dessert in England long before George I, but it had disappeared under (you guessed it) Oliver Cromwell. Perhaps because it had been dubbed by the Puritans a "lewd custom," the pudding never quite attained its former glory – not even after the Restoration. That is, not until it was served to George I – forever remembered as "The Pudding King" – on that fateful Christmas day in 1714.

Of course, no discussion of Christmas would be complete without some mention of presents. The best royal gifts in history range from the mundane (George VI of Britain supposedly gave away "hundreds of plate warmers" as Christmas gifts in the 1940s) to the ridiculous (Louis IX of France gave Henry III of England a live elephant). Similarly, stories of Christmas spirit and Christmas scroogery exist in equal proportion. Among the most touching stories, in her book "The Royal Jewels," Suzy Menkes tells how Queen Alexandra gave a footman, who had already received his standard Christmas gift, a pair of gold cufflinks, simply because he was feeling lonely. At the other extreme, Henry VIII let it be known that he was through once and for all with his estranged wife, Catherine of Aragon, when he returned to her the Christmas gifts she sent him in 1531.

Finally, for lovers of "On This Day" history: Charlemagne was crowned Holy Roman Emperor on Dec. 25th, 800; William, Duke of Normandy, was crowned King of England on Dec. 25th, 1066; and the Empress Elizabeth of Russia died on Dec. 25th, 1761.

LITTLE PEOPLE AT ROYAL COURTS

Mention dwarfs and most people immediately think of Snow White, but dwarfs were a staple at most every royal court in history, and the courts of Britain were no exception. From the tales of Tom Thumb at the court of the legendary King Arthur to Coppernin, a German dwarf in the service of George III's mother, Augusta, Princess of Wales, and the last court dwarf in England, dwarfs were just another part of court life in the British Isles.

Unfortunately, court dwarfs are today frequently overlooked as the mere amusements of historical royalty; and while many were just that, several others managed to carve out a significant place for themselves at court and in history. Not least among these were three dwarfs (or "little people" in the modern vernacular) who started their careers at the court of King Charles I and Queen Henrietta Maria.

The first and most well-known of these three little people was Jeffrey (or Geoffrey) Hudson, who was born in 1619 in Oakham, which is located in – of all places – England's smallest county, Rutland, in the East Midlands. Jeffrey's parents were both of normal size and his father was a butcher who served George Villiers, the 1st Duke of Buckingham, as keeper of his baiting bulls. While the diminutive boy may have served as a page in the Duke of Buckingham's household, it's certain that he performed a more dramatic, if not demeaning, role in 1626 that changed the course of his life.

Major events had taken place the previous year, including the death of James VI of Scotland and I of England, the succession of his son, Charles I, on March 27, 1625, and the marriage of the new king to the 15-year-old French Princess Henrietta Maria just a few months later. Sometime after Charles' coronation in February 1626, the new king and queen visited Charles' favorite courtier, the Duke of Buckingham, at his country estate of Burley-on-the-Hill in Rutland, where they were thrown a lavish banquet. During the meal, a large cold pie – or "coffin" – was placed before the king and queen, but before the pie could be cut, an 18-inch man in a suit of armor burst out from the crust, stood before the queen and bowed.

The little "man" was 7-year-old Jeffrey Hudson and he had played his role so well that the Duke of Buckingham gifted him to the enraptured queen, who made him a part of her entourage. But rather than simply serving as a court fool, Jeffrey became a trusted confidante of the queen and was soon dubbed "Lord Minimus" or "Sir" Jeffrey. The relationship between the two is perhaps not surprising when considered within the context of Henrietta Maria's early life at the English court.

Almost from day one, her relationships with both her adopted country and her husband were strained. As a Catholic, she was looked upon with suspicion by the government and the people of England – a situation that precluded her from being at her husband's side during his coronation. Not that he seemed to want her there anyway. For his part, Charles appears to have found her far less interesting than the Duke of Buckingham, under whose control he largely resided. To make matters worse, early in their marriage, the king forced Henrietta Maria to send back many of her French servants, allowing her only her chaplain and two ladies-in-waiting, leaving a gap of friendly human contact for the queen that must have been filled nicely by Jeffrey.

By the time of the 1st Duke of Buckingham's death in 1628 – which opened the door for a better relationship between Charles and Henrietta Maria – Jeffrey was firmly established as a court favorite of the queen. During his 18 years as Henrietta Maria's companion, Jeffrey made a name for himself in London society and had a number of unique experiences, including performing in a Ben Jonson masque and fighting in at least one duel. His status was important enough that he was even sent as an emissary to France to find a suitable mid-wife for the queen. He was also painted by a number of artists, including Sir Anthony Van Dyck, who, in 1633, painted 14-year-old Jeffrey with 24-year-old Henrietta Maria. At the time of the painting, it seems likely that Jeffrey was still only a diminutive 18 inches tall, a height he maintained until he was 30, when he suddenly grew to his full height of around three feet, nine inches. But the year that saw Jeffrey's growth spurt, 1649, also found him in far different circumstances than when Van Dyck painted him with the queen.

In 1644, during the English Civil War, Jeffrey escaped with Henrietta Maria to France, although his service to her in her exiled court did not last out the year. History tells us that in the fall of that year, Jeffrey engaged in another duel, which, like the first, had been prompted by remarks about his size. This second critical duel was fought on horseback – a measure meant to put Jeffrey at roughly the same level as his opponent – with a man named Crofts, who apparently hadn't taken the duel seriously and arrived armed only with a "squirt" or water gun, and ended when Jeffrey shot and killed him. As a result, he was forced to leave not only Henrietta Maria, but also France. It is here where the relatively scarce accounts of Jeffrey's history seem to go awry, but his adventures, and misadventures, can be summed up with the following...

Between his departure from Henrietta Maria in 1644 and his death in 1682, Jeffrey fought in the English Civil War as a Captain of Horse, serving with enough valor to earn him the nickname of "Strenuous Jeffrey." He was captured by Turkish pirates and spent 25 years in slavery before returning to England and living off a pension provided by the 2nd Duke of Buckingham. Finally, in 1676, he was living in London at the restored royal court, but was soon accused of participating in a Papist plot, which landed him in prison, where he died in 1682 at the age of 63.

As is often the case, an ignominious end appears to have brought Jeffrey a more enduring remembrance than many of his peers. Sir Walter Scott wrote about Jeffrey and his adventures in "Peveril of the Peak" in 1822. More recently, Oakham Ales – a brew-pub based in Peterborough but founded in Oakham – created Jeffrey Hudson Bitter (or JHB), which has won several awards, in honor of the dwarf.

In addition, the six foot, nine inch author Michael Crichton ironically (and seemingly intentionally) used the pseudonym Jeffrey Hudson during the very early stages of his writing career. Modern visitors to Oakham can still also be seen the 17th century thatched cottage where Jeffrey was born.

In life at least, two of Charles and Henrietta Maria's other court dwarfs fared better than poor Jeffrey, although their relative lack of infamy is reflected in the accordingly sparse information available about them today. The first of these,

Richard Gibson, was also a court painter of miniatures. As ironic as that may sound, Richard's artistic talent was not a mere amusement, but rather was quite good and much admired. In fact, one of his miniature paintings, a depiction of the Biblical Parable of the Lost Sheep, was so valued by Charles I that the keeper of royal pictures, Abraham Van der Doort, committed suicide when he thought he had lost it.

Richard was born in Cumberland, England in 1615 and later became a page in a stately home in Mortlake (in what is now a part of the Greater London Borough of Richmond upon Thames), where his artistic talent was first discovered. The lady of the house apparently felt his talent was sufficient to place him under the instruction of a Mr. Francis Cleyn, who was the manager of the Mortlake Tapestry Works. It's not quite clear exactly when Richard came into the court of Charles I, but when he did he served the court in the capacity of a page, at least until his artistic talent became predominant. Sometime around the mid to late 1630s, Henrietta Maria encouraged Richard to marry the third court dwarf in our story, Anne Shepherd.

Even less is known of Anne than is of Richard, but we do know that she was born in 1620 and was about the same height as her betrothed – approximately three feet, ten inches tall. Her official role at court was in the usual capacity of page, but she appears to have developed some sort of a bond with Lady Mary Villiers, daughter of the 1st Duke of Buckingham. It was a relationship that seems to have mimicked that of Henrietta Maria and Jeffrey Hudson and, indeed, another portrait by Van Dyck entitled, "Lady Mary Villiers with Mrs. Gibson, her Dwarf," and painted around the late 1630s, enforces this idea. The similarities not only in the subject matter of the two paintings, but also in the poses of Henrietta Maria and Mary and their respective dwarfs are understandable since Mary and her siblings grew up at the court of Charles I after the death of their father in 1628. The young Mary was most certainly under the tutelage of Henrietta Maria and was known to emulate the queen in many ways.

In the wedding of the two court dwarfs, the king gave the bride away, the queen presented Anne with a diamond ring, and the poet Edmund Waller commemorated the marriage in a poem entitled, "Of the Marriage of the Dwarfs." Part of the poem reads:

Thrice happy is that humble pair,
Beneath the level of all care!
Over whose heads those arrows fly
Of sad distrust and jealousy;
Secured in as high extreme,
As if the world held none but them. (7-12)

Although the marriage of Richard and Anne appears to have been "arranged," it was a happy one, and the couple had nine children of normal size, although only five survived to adulthood. At least three of the children inherited their father's talents and became artists themselves, including Susan Penelope Rosse (1652-1700), who was also a painter of miniatures.

Richard must have also displayed skill in the art of diplomacy during the English Civil War and the Interregnum, since he earned the respect of Oliver Cromwell, whom he painted on several occasions. Upon the Restoration, Richard returned to the royal courts – first with Charles II, then with James II, where he became drawing master to the Princesses Mary and Anne.

Finally, when Princess Mary married the Prince of Orange in 1677, Richard (and, presumably, Anne) went with her and remained at her court until about 1688, shortly before she succeeded to the British throne. Richard died in London on July 23rd, 1690 at the age of 75, and Anne died in 1709 at the age of 89 (some accounts claim she died before Richard, at the age of 80), and they were buried together at St. Paul's Church in Covent Garden.

While Richard and Anne may have escaped the tragic fate of Jeffrey Hudson, at least one story about Richard Gibson seems to indicate that talent at the English court didn't always consistently equate to full-blown respect. It seems that Gibson was also made to jump out of a pie, after which he had to walk across the table displaying portraits of the king and queen, which he had copied onto playing cards from Van Dyck's paintings. Nevertheless, Richard's legacy lives on today in the miniature paintings he created – many of which he signed using the initials D.G. for either "Dick" or "Dwarf" Gibson – as well as in a number of paintings *of* him, including several by Sir Peter Lely. One of Lely's paintings, "Gibson and his Wife," depicts Richard and Anne together holding hands.

Tangentially, it seems that Charles and Henrietta Maria also had a court giant, William Evans, who was reportedly around eight feet tall. Each time he came to court, William carried a dwarf in his pocket because it "amused" the king. Little other information is readily available about William, but it's possible that he was a Welshman who lived between 1599 and 1634 and was originally a porter to Charles I's father, King James I of England. It's also possible that the dwarf he carried in his pocket was Jeffrey Hudson, since at least one or two contemporary images existed of William and Jeffrey together.

Perhaps the final irony in all of this is that Charles I is listed in the Guinness Book of World's Records as Britain's shortest king (Queen Victoria holds the record for the shortest British monarch). Most accounts suggest that he was between five feet and five feet, four inches tall. Henrietta Maria was also short, with most estimates placing her at five feet or under. Although many people will point to the fact that, in general, people were shorter "back then," both the king and queen were still remarkably short for their time.

As for Charles and Henrietta Maria's three court dwarfs, they may have gotten their places at the royal court thanks to their unusually small size, but they certainly made their own places in history through their adventures and talents. In the end, the motto of Rutland, Jeffrey Hudson's birthplace, perhaps sums up their stories the best – *"multum in parvo"* or "much in little."

An Unusual Journey Through Royal History

THE REAL AND SURREAL ROYALS

The National Portrait Gallery in London has some really beautiful and important paintings of the British royal family. It also has a few that are perhaps a bit more, shall we say, "eclectic."

On a visit several years ago, I was admiring the many exquisite portraits of the historical and modern royal family when I suddenly came across a gigantic portrait that momentarily stopped me dead in my tracks. Mind you, I firmly believe that art is a purely personal matter and am as open-minded as the next person, but my initial thought was one of complete dislike.

The portrait – painted by John Wonnacott and unveiled in 2000 in celebration of the 100th birthday of The Queen Mother – made the six most important members of the royal family, four corgis and the White Drawing Room of Buckingham Palace look like they were melting off the canvas. After quickly noting how miserably unhappy Prince William looked and that the corgis were larger than Prince Phllip, I turned on my heel to walk away.

Before I could make it to the stairs, however, a kindly docent stopped me to remark that I had not given the portrait ample consideration, then proceeded to present me with a complete and thorough analysis of the portrait's finer points. Among the most interesting aspects of my lesson, I learned that

Prince Charles is wearing a dress shoe on his left foot and a house slipper on his right foot, while one of the seams of the gigantic portrait cuts directly through his crotch. He also pointed out that Prince Harry's left arm is that of a grown man rather than a teenage boy, and something resembling a roller skate is painted into the carpet.

Needless to say, I was converted and began to find the portrait fascinating. I went so far as to buy a postcard of the portrait to keep for myself and even made a diary entry of the docent's comments and my own thoughts. Since then, I've thought about and looked at the portrait many times and have increasingly found it intriguing less for the presence of the surreal touches and more for the accurate portrayal of the subject matter. Not that anyone except The Queen Mother looks completely normal, as the fishbowl effect of the portrait distorts everything except the central subject. No, the realism of the portrait is more in the presentation of the roles and positions of the royals it portrays.

To begin with, Prince Philip is confined to the far distance of the portrait, slightly apart from the others with his face to the ground and a somewhat enigmatic grin. I laughingly wonder whether he had just made one of his infamous gaffes and was ordered by The Queen to stand back and consider his behavior. In all seriousness, his position in the portrait seems to be an obvious reference to his position in the family. As the husband of The Queen, his importance is merely tangential. As the father of the heir, he has served his purpose and now it's the corgis, at the front of the picture, who share The Queen's chamber.

Unlike Prince Philip, The Queen, Prince Charles and Prince Harry all make up the center portion of the picture, surrounding The Queen Mother, who sits gracefully on a yellow sofa. Little can be said of The Queen, other than that her head is located in almost the dead center of the portrait and she is looking lovingly down on her mother, whose back is to her. As dutiful a daughter, I suppose, as she is a queen.

For her part, The Queen Mother looks at her undoubted favorite, Prince Charles, who likewise gazes back at her. The Queen Mother's arm is extended toward Charles and her hand is lightly closed as if she's handing him something. Obviously, it wasn't something he really needed, like his matching shoe or wise advice on how to be a beloved member of the royal family.

As to Charles' mismatched footwear, I am firmly of the opinion that it says something about his conflicting nature as a person and a member of the royal family. On the one hand (or foot, in this case), his personality is like the dress shoe, formal and traditional – the side of him that is committed to royal duty and carrying on the family traditions. On the other hand, the slipper represents the more relaxed and flexible aspects of his personality – the side of him that likes to garden and state his opinion about a plethora of subjects in a somewhat "unprincely" fashion. I will not even begin to speculate whether or not the seam through Charles' crotch has any deeper meaning.

In typical fashion, Prince Harry leans over the back of the chair in which his great-grandmother is seated and looks as though he is in thoroughly jolly spirits. He is the only person in the picture who is either not standing upright or positioned in any relative royal dignity. On a cursory glance at Harry's face, it's easy to think that he is looking at The Queen Mother, but a closer inspection reveals that he is not. Personally, it seems to me that he is looking at Prince William's shoes or maybe the back end of one of the corgis. Why he would be looking at either one of these instead of his great-grandmother, I'm not sure, although

I fancy his gaze represents either a lack of focus typical in a 15-year-old boy or his relatively carefree position among the party at hand.

Prince William, on the other hand, seems to be carrying not only the weight of his now and future position, but also the sorrows of the past. As the largest and most dominant figure in the portrait, the symbolism is that he is the hope and glory of the royal family is blatantly obvious. With his hands in his pocket, his face slanted forlornly toward the floor, and a look of abject sadness on his face, he is neither enjoying his own importance and glory, nor is he completely satisfied with the present company alone. As no one in the portrait is paying any attention to William, Wonnacott leaves it entirely to the viewer to sympathize with him, a strategy that worked quite effectively on me.

Granted, all of this is my interpretation, both of what the artist intended and of the royals themselves, but it certainly seems to me that this otherwise strangely surreal portrait is a more accurate reflection of the real people we venerate as royalty than the hundreds of more classic and formal portraits that permeate our collective consciousness. Personally, although I will always continue to be more aesthetically pleased by the classic portraits that represent royalty as flawless, near-divine creatures, I will never again dismiss so quickly portraits like Wonnacott's that so skillfully capture the human and fallible side of the royal family.

The King's Evil

In 1712, the scrofulous two-year-old son of a Staffordshire bookseller was brought to London for presentation to Queen Anne. On seeing the diseased child and the swollen and leaking sores on his neck, the queen – resplendent in glittering diamonds and a long black hood – leaned down and carefully stroked the boy's cheeks and throat with her bare hands before presenting him with a special gold coin, or touchpiece. The boy and his family returned to Staffordshire, no doubt anticipating the boy's miraculous return to health thanks to the queen's divine touch.

In spite of temporary partial blindness and permanent scars left on his face by the scrofula that plagued his childhood, Dr. Samuel Johnson wore the touchpiece given to him by the queen for the rest of his life. Despite Anne's failure to cure Dr. Johnson, many contemporaries claimed that she and other monarchs in France and England did in fact have the power to heal, simply by touch.

Although the concept has long had much broader religious and spiritual connotations as the "laying on of hands" – a philosophy the early Christian's based on ancient Jewish beliefs, it first extended to European monarchs in 11th century France, with England following shortly thereafter. As always, however, there was a little matter of one-upsmanship between the two countries, with each claiming they were the first to possess healing powers. French legend perpetuated that Clovis (d. 511), founder of the French kingdom, was the first to employ the "Divine Touch" (also known as the "King's Touch" or "Royal Touch"), solidly routing the English, who claimed Edward the Confessor (d. 1066) was the first in that country. The truth of the matter is that France's Robert II the Pious (d. 1031) was really the first – undoubtedly a win for the French, but only by a hair.

In any case, both countries seemed to have justified the continuation of the power in successive monarchs in the same way – divine right as a legitimate French or English monarch descended from either Robert the Pious or Edward the Confessor, and anointment with pure chrism (holy oil consecrated by a bishop), rather than plain old sacred oil. Backed by these credentials – not to mention the Roman Catholic Church – the belief was perpetuated, almost unbroken, into the 18th and 19th centuries.

But the tradition did not go unchanged. Initially, the power to heal was applied to most all diseases, but was eventually applied primarily to scrofula – a form of tuberculosis that affects lymph nodes in the neck. Because of the application of the King's Touch to this particular affliction, the disease became known as *"le mal du roi"* or "The King's Evil." The ceremony of "Touching for the King's Evil" also changed over the years and varied between the two countries. In both countries, however, the monarch often performed the act at large ceremonies on important holy days. On Easter, 1686, for instance, Louis XIV of France is said to have touched 1,600 people at a ceremony at Versailles, repeating the words "The King toucheth thee; the Lord healteth thee," with each person.

Not to be outdone, in Britain, Charles II, reportedly touched between 90,000 and 100,000 or more people during his reign. And, no, those figures do not include attractive women.

At this point in English history, the demand for the King's Touch was so high that special application certificates were established as a prerequisite to participation.

Perhaps like many aspects of Charles II's reign, his ability to perform with enthusiasm so many traditional rituals of the monarchy was directly tied to the need to re-inspire a sense of awe for the monarchy, which had been lost in the Civil War and during the Republic. Ironically, it was Charles' grandfather and the first Stuart monarch of England, James I, who first tried to put an end to the custom, calling it superstitious. He was not fully successful, but he sparked off years of waxing and waning popularity of the tradition in England, which finally ended once and for all with the last of the Stuart monarchs, Queen Anne, in 1714. In between, William III was just one of those who waned. Like James I, he considered the practice superstitious and refused to perform the act, with one unique exception. Perhaps under pressure, the King reportedly touched an afflicted person and said, "God give you better health and more sense."

As for his successor, Queen Anne, she seems to have taken on the responsibility with incredible conviction, although her success was both touted and questioned. While contemporary surgeons, not to mention newly healthy subjects, claimed the queen's touch was efficacious, others regarded that her questionable legitimacy as queen also put her healing powers in doubt.

By the same argument, the exiled Stuart's – both the Old Pretender and the Young Pretender – continued to perform the act for a great many petitioners. In fact, word has it that the unbelieving William III even referred petitioners he turned away to his vanquished rivals.

After Queen Anne's death and the discontinuation of the Royal Touch by the Hanoverian monarchs in Britain, the practice continued in earnest in France. As in England, however, the Revolution brought the practice to a halt, only to have it reinstated in 1815 for the practical reason of "strengthening the monarchy, if not of healing the sick." Clearly, it did neither, and Charles X performed the last ceremony in France on May 31st, 1825.

The disappearance of touching for the king's evil was probably just as much a result of an increasing understanding of science and medicine as it was of the decreasing God-like reverence of monarchs. But, even today, it would be silly to completely disregard the idea of the healing power of royalty. Scientifically, of course, there's little reason to believe that the touch of any person can actually heal an illness, but modern royals have proven over the years that a simple touch can not only change the life of a person with a terrible disease or affliction, but can also change the attitudes of those who are healthy.

Diana, Princess of Wales is most frequently credited with having applied this "healing touch" to patients with HIV and AIDS – bringing hope to their lives and understanding about the nature of the illness to the public at large, but other royals have done the same for equally worthy causes. In 1956, for example, Queen Elizabeth II broke convention when she shook hands with patients at a leper colony in Nigeria. Her touch may not have healed those people of their affliction, but, in a far less ceremonious and more personal way, she did exactly what English and French monarchs had been doing since the 11th century – momentarily closed the gap between the fortunate and the unfortunate.

An Unusual Journey Through Royal History

THE OFFBEAT LEGACY OF ROYAL EPONYMS

Every American child learns in grammar school that Virginia was named for the "Virgin" Queen Elizabeth I of England, Charleston originated as Charles Town in honor of King Charles II, and Georgia was named after King George II. Of course, Queen Victoria's legacy is as vast as her empire once was. Cities, islands, waterfalls, lakes, rivers, universities, museums, and architecture, just to name a few, are all named for the queen who gave her name to an era.

Between places, ships, and, of course, buildings, there is no doubt that the names of Britain's royals are forever imprinted on our collective consciousness, but apart from the historical and obvious royal eponyms, there are many more that we are not as familiar with. Even among those we are familiar with, we may not know how the names came to be eponymous.

There's a wonderful anecdote about how the *RMS Queen Mary* was named. Apparently, The Cunard Line planned to name the ship the *Queen Victoria*, but when the company went to George V and told him that they wanted to name the ship after Britain's "greatest queen," the king responded by saying something to the effect of, 'my wife will be delighted.' To save any embarrassment, the ship was duly named the *Queen Mary*.

Accidentally or not, Britain's queens have always inspired eponyms, especially among the sweeter things in life. Unlike in France, the connection between Britain's queens and cakes has been a more positive one. When a famous Polish pianist served Queen Elizabeth The Queen Mother a flourless chocolate cake, he couldn't possibly have imagined that she would like it so much she would ask for the recipe; but she did and served it to her own guests whenever possible. Fittingly, the cake is now known as The Queen Mother's Cake.

Likewise, history tells us that you can thank Queen Charlotte for the Apple Charlotte. George III's consort is not only credited with inspiring the layered apple cake, but, sometimes, with actually bringing the recipe with her from Germany. But even if the recipe wasn't in her trousseau, it is certain that the apple-loving Queen Consort did introduce to Britain a number of new apple varieties from Germany, including one that's named for her.

But royal ladies didn't always have to do so much to inspire an eponym. Another royal consort made her name synonymous with wild carrot, the plant we know better as Queen Anne's Lace, simply by wearing the flowers of the plant. This particular Queen Anne – Anne of Denmark, the wife of James I – was simply doing what so many more modern royals have done… start an eponymous fashion trend.

Perhaps the most famous of these is the Windsor Knot – a style of tying a necktie that creates a thicker, wider knot than usual. Credited to the Duke of Windsor, the origin of the eponym is perhaps just as controversial as the Duke himself was. Like so many other eponyms, the origin of the Windsor Knot is disputed, and the Duke of Windsor himself dismissed that he had invented it. And speaking of eponymous controversy, it would be irresponsible not to point out that even poor Queen Charlotte's claim to the Apple Charlotte is not without dispute.

Some say that the name of the cake actually originates from "charlets," meat dishes that were popular in the 15th century.

While some eponyms may be simply disputed, others lean towards the apocryphal, like the idea that the Bloody Mary cocktail was named for England's "Bloody Mary," Queen Mary I of England. While cocktail history is (appropriately) somewhat clouded and contradictory at times, a commonly told story claims that a Parisian bartender created the drink and named it after a girl he knew at Chicago's Bucket of Blood Club.

If you think that explanation is a bit strange, consider for a moment the piercing named for Prince Albert, who, legend tells us, had a very intimate part of his anatomy pierced so that he could "control" it underneath the tight-fitting trousers of the time. Again, the story is perhaps dubious, but it certainly has a firm place in today's alternative popular culture.

One thing is sure about royal eponyms – the most interesting ones are those you didn't learn about in school.

An Unusual Journey Through Royal History

CHIEFLY ROYAL RELATIONS

It never fails to happen. In America, at presidential election time, genealogists scour the past to give the potential Commanders in Chief a royal lineage. Despite America's love of democracy, we still seem to revel in royal connections for our elected leaders.

Back in 2004, the world's news media picked up on the story that Democratic presidential candidate John Kerry had significant genealogical links to European royalty and aristocracy. But far from attempting to create romantic notions reminiscent of the Kennedy era and America's "Camelot," the purpose of the media frenzy appeared to be much more practical, perhaps even tactical.

With Election Day drawing near, the news that had previously attracted only the likes of royal watchers now became geared towards voters, with most of the reports focusing on the theory (courtesy of Burke's Peerage) that – historically speaking – presidential races are usually won by the most "royal" of the candidates. For instance, they cite that George W. Bush – a distant cousin of Queen Elizabeth II – beat Al Gore, who reportedly had fewer royal blood ties than his opponent, thanks to the "royalty factor."

Of course, some might say that Bush, like The Queen, was not actually voted into office the first time, while others might point to the fact that, also like The Queen, he (very nearly) succeeded his father into office. In Bush's case, it could even be said that the relationship with his brother – then governor of Florida – was more critical in winning the presidency than distant relationships to European royalty. But I digress.

As fascinating as it is to consider how royal connections could potentially sway American political decisions, I personally find the relationships between American Commanders in Chief and European royalty – both genealogical and political – much more interesting. After all, if it wasn't for George Washington's lack of interest in a royal title, America might today have a king instead of a president.

The choice to forgo a monarchy, it seems, was the right one for America. When Washington was elected President of the United States in 1789, the Holy Roman Empire still existed, France had a king, Russia had a tsar, China had an emperor and Japan had a shogun –none of which exist today. Even European rulers of the time recognized Washington's foresightedness and integrity. When he refused to run for a third term as president, opting to retire his power in 1797, Britain's King George III is reported to have said that if Washington could truly give up his power voluntarily, he was "the greatest man in the world." Around the time of his death, the exiled Napoleon is said to have mused, "They expected me to be another Washington."

But even Washington had been born a subject of Britain. In fact, the first seven presidents of the United States were born as British subjects. The eighth, Martin Van Buren, was the first US president born after the American Revolution and, therefore, the first president who was born an American citizen. Ironically, Van Buren was also one of the first presidents not to come from a predominantly British background. Unlike his predecessors, he was of mainly Dutch heritage.

Historically speaking, however, very few other American presidents come from anything other than predominantly British ancestry. In fact, according to Burke's Peerage, 37 of the 44 (one American president served two non-consecutive terms) presidents can trace their ancestry back to England, Scotland, Ireland or Wales. It comes as no surprise then that most of those 44 presidents can also trace their family history to some member of royalty, especially when you consider that genealogists believe that all people with European ancestry alive today are probably descended from Charlemagne, the first Holy Roman Emperor.

Similarly, some experts believe that as much as half the population of Britain is descended from William the Conqueror, automatically making all such people distant relations of royalty. Not surprising then that some amateur genealogists claim that as many as 20 US presidents are descended from the man who was also infamously known as William the Bastard. Of course, the relationship between these presidents and their royal ancestor – if it is indisputable – is quite distant. For most of them, their rise to power perhaps had more to do with their nearer relations, as the U.S. has had five sets of near relations serve as president – none more distant than fifth cousins. (Kerry and Bush are themselves 9th cousins twice removed – closer than each man's individual relationship to Queen Elizabeth II.)

One thing is for certain, royal relation or no, the majority of American presidents have shared at least one of two other traits with their royal cousins – powerful families or money – assets that, on the whole, have undoubtedly helped them enormously when building relations with their royal counterparts (although it didn't do 4th president James Madison much good when the British Army chased him out of Washington D.C. during the War of 1812). By the Victorian Era, relations were so good between American presidents and British royalty that 15th president James Buchanan reportedly slept in the hallway of the White House to better accommodate the Prince of Wales' entourage in 1860. Twenty years later, Queen Victoria presented 19th president Rutherford B. Hayes with a desk carved from the timbers of the H.M.S. Resolute. This brings us back to modern times. The "Resolute Desk" – given to a US president by an ancestor of Queen Elizabeth II – is still in the Oval Office of the White House and is currently being used by President Barack Obama who, although is perhaps singular as America's first African-American president, does have his share of royal genealogical connections (for one, he is a 16th cousin once removed from Queen Elizabeth II). And since back in 2004, incumbent President George W. Bush – 13th cousin twice removed of Queen Elizabeth II – won the election against his slightly less royally-connected rival, John Kerry - half 12th cousin twice removed of The Queen - it seems that the "royalty factor" may indeed have merit.

An Unusual Journey Through Royal History

QUEEN OF WHERE ELSE?

Britain's Queen Elizabeth II is the owner of dozens of inherited titles, but is she also in the line of succession to any other European throne? This question was asked of me when I was writing a regular column on the modern and historical royals. I had a few inklings, but nothing substantial to go by. Meanwhile, my correspondent wrote to Buckingham Palace to see if they had the answer. The response – "We don't know" – sent me spinning into a frenzy of excitement and research.

To begin with, one of Queen Elizabeth II's many titles is Duke of Normandy (yes, *duke*), although the title only applies to her in the Channel Islands. The title harkens back to William, Duke of Normandy, who we know best as William the Conqueror. After he won his claim to the English crown in 1066, his descendants were both monarchs of England and dukes of Normandy – that is until England lost everything except the Channel Islands to France in the early 13th century. I mention this both as an interesting aside and to eliminate in advance any potential misconception that, through this title, The Queen is actually a pretender to the duchy of Normandy.

That little detail aside, how do we begin to determine if The Queen is in the line of succession to any other European throne? One way is to study the lineage of each of the spouses of the British monarchs (or almost monarchs) who are direct ancestors of Elizabeth II. (For reasons that are too numerous to name, I am only going as far back as James VI of Scotland and I of England.) It's important to remember that not all British monarchs are direct ancestors of The Queen – for example, The Queen is not a descendant of either George IV or William IV – nor have all her direct ancestors been monarchs – George III's father, Frederick, Prince of Wales, never became king, nor did Queen Victoria's father, Edward, Duke of Kent.

Keeping in mind that I am certainly not a professional genealogist, my method was to study (to a reasonable extent) the ancestors and descendants of both the paternal and maternal line of the spouses to determine probable existing connections. Given the limited amount of time and other factors, I do not claim that I am exactly correct in my assessments and assumptions or that I have researched each and every possibility (because there are virtually endless possibilities). Instead, I give you my honest attempt at an answer, in semi-chronological order.

The best I can figure is that The Queen's strongest claim – at least in terms of the line of succession – to any other throne is in Denmark, where she actually has at least two strong connections. In 1589, James I of England married Anne of Demark, daughter of Frederick II of Denmark. Although both Queen Margrethe II of Denmark and Elizabeth II are descended from Frederick II, any right Queen Elizabeth might have to the succession thanks to this relationship is likely to be so watered down it would be virtually impossible. In any case, she has a more recent claim through Edward VII's wife, Alexandra of Denmark, whose father, Christian IX of Denmark, was the great-great-great grandfather of Queen Margrethe. This makes Queen Elizabeth and Queen Margrethe third cousins once removed. If this connection does indeed give her a valid place in the line of succession to the Danish throne, I would imagine her place is very low on the list.

Skip over a few generations that don't directly apply to this situation and you get to the Georges, most of whom married minor German princesses who didn't bring a whole lot in the way of major royal houses.

Although Sophia Dorothea of Brunswick-Celle was George I's wife, she was not the first Hanoverian queen of Britain, as George had divorced her before ascending to the throne. Regardless, she was still the mother of George II and, in that way, provides Elizabeth II with a more significant – albeit very distant – claim to another royal house: Prussia (or, if you like, Germany). Sophia Dorothea's maternal grandmother was the daughter of Magdalene Hohenzollern of Brandenburg – herself the daughter of John George Hohenzollern, Elector of Brandenburg, who is the direct ancestor of the last German emperor (king of Prussia), Frederick William IV. Since the connection is several hundred years old and the monarchy in Germany was dissolved during World War I, it's reasonable to assume that it would be a cold day in hell before Queen Elizabeth ever got anywhere near that particular throne.

My correspondent pointed out another possibility related to George II through his daughter Anne, the Princess Royal (d. 1759), although technically passed on to Elizabeth II through her grandmother, Queen Mary (Princess May of Teck). Anne married Willem IV, Prince of Orange, who is the direct ancestor of Queen Beatrix of the Netherlands. Thanks to Queen Mary's ancestry through Anne and Willem's daughter, Wilhelmina Caroline, Elizabeth II is also Willem's descendant. This complex relationship is just one example of the many distant familial connections that can be easily overlooked.

Without going blind studying each and every one of the various branches of the seemingly endless numbers of minor German royalty, my understanding is that the next three female Georgian ancestors of Elizabeth II brought little to the table. George II's wife, Caroline of Brandenburg-Anspach, and George III's wife, Sophia Charlotte of Mecklenburg-Strelitz, actually sandwiched in the more interesting of the three women – Augusta of Saxe-Gotha-Altenburg, wife of Frederick, Prince of Wales, and mother of George III. To be specific, it is Augusta's bloodline that is interesting. Although she was never queen herself, Augusta has the distinction of being both great grandmother to Queen Victoria and great aunt to Prince Albert. Frederick II's son (Augusta's brother) was Frederick III of Saxe-Gotha-Altenburg – the direct ancestor of Prince Albert (of Saxe-Coburg-Gotha) through Albert's mother. Therefore, Victoria and Albert's direct common ancestor was their great-great grandfather, Frederick II of Saxe-Gotha-Altenburg, Augusta and Frederick III's father. But, as we know, Victoria and Albert were also first cousins through her mother, Victoria of Saxe-Coburg, and his father, Ernest I, Duke of Saxe-Coburg-Saalfeld, who were siblings.

Although this particular aspect of Elizabeth II's family history really means very little in terms of Elizabeth II's position in the line of succession to another European royal house, it does make one point crystal clear – Elizabeth II is related as much to herself as she is to anyone else (I say with tongue in cheek). In all honesty, however, I think this is the essence of our attempts to understand and make sense of the complexities of the British and European royal houses. It's the knowledge that centuries of inter-marriage among all the various royals has forged a virtually unbreakable blood bond that means each monarch may have not only more than their primary claim to their own throne, but distant claims to other thrones as well.

While Queen Elizabeth II is about as unlikely to ascend to any other royal throne as I am, it's at least fun to consider the possibilities.

A Pageant of Queens

As revelations of royal women resorting to Botox injections become commonplace and speculation over their rumored "nips and tucks" begins to reach even mainstream press, it's almost comforting to learn that even the famously lovely ancient Egyptian Queen Nefertiti – whose name roughly translates to "the beautiful one is come" – resorted to an early form of facelift to improve or maintain her looks. But if anything ties modern royal women striving for eternal physical beauty, such as Sarah, Duchess of York, Princess Michael of Kent and Queen Silvia of Sweden, together with famous royal women of the past – aside from their royal titles, of course – it's the desire to be, or at least look, young and beautiful.

In fact, the direct correlation between beauty and royal women, namely princesses and queens, is not only timeless, but deeply rooted in our collective psyche, just as it has been for thousands of years. You don't have to think very long or hard over history to find evidence of how this idea has been so permanently cemented in our minds. Turn to classical history and literature and you immediately encounter Helen of Troy, wife of the King of Sparta and the woman whose face "launched a thousand ships."

Or, if the classics aren't your style, pick up any book of fairy tales and you're sure to find at least a few stories where the heroine is a beautiful princess. Naturally, there are never any ugly princesses and even the evil queens are beautiful – although they are usually worried about rapidly approaching age and the subsequent deterioration of their looks.

Legendary, and perhaps exaggerated, accounts of classical beauty and fanciful ideals of the stereotypical lovely and gentle fairy tale princess aside, there is little doubt that the queens and princesses of both modern and historical times have always been held to a higher standard than "normal" women. After all, before there were models and movie stars, there were royal women and, just as today, they were expected to play the part.

A wonderful anecdote of the expectations of queenly beauty is given in "My Blue Notebooks," the diary of the 19th century French courtesan Liane de Pougy, who later became Princess Georges Ghika. Known for her exquisite beauty and terminal elegance, Liane tells how, in 1892 or 1893, French dramatist Henri Meilhac asked her to attend a performance at the *Opéra-Comique* in Paris and emphatically insisted that she wear her "tiara, masses of jewels, a low-cut dress... [and] white cloak with the gold embroidery and the ermine lining." He also told her she "must have an entourage" and that she "must arrive before the curtain goes up." For her troubles, he gave Liane 2000 francs and promised her the left stage box, but failed to provide an explanation for her dramatic appearance and entrance.

Liane did as she was asked and made a grand entrance to her box at the opera promptly 15 minutes before the curtain rose, dressed to the nines and accompanied by two equally elegant and well-dressed ladies. Much to her surprise, every person in the packed opera house rose to their feet and turned to look at her. The orchestra suddenly "broke into patriotic music," causing Liane and her entourage to rise to their feet and prompting the audience to break into spontaneous applause. The celebrated courtesan went gracefully along with the strange situation, assuming that the display was simply a "homage to my youth and beauty."

Within moments, Meilhac entered Liane's box and, hysterical with laughter, explained what had just happened... "We're expecting the Queen of Sweden – in the box opposite – they thought you were her, it's too killing for words." Liane looked across to the other box and saw: "a lanky, sad-looking woman, rather badly dressed, surrounded by quite an entourage. Her entrance had been ruined, no one noticed it. It was me... to whom the crowd had paid homage – and the orchestra too, because it was the Swedish national anthem that they had played."

Meilhac summed up the situation best when he said later, "Homage to beauty! *Vox populi, vox dei* [trans: The voice of the people is the voice of God]! How beautiful is our Liane! That is how people expect a queen to look, and she has proved it."

While the incident was clearly a set-up, it does demonstrate that the public expects at least to be sparkled and awed by the splendid attire and accoutrements of royal women, if not by their dazzling beauty. One modern queen who knew this all too well was Queen Elizabeth The Queen Mother. When her husband, George VI, unexpectedly came to the British throne in 1936, the new monarchs were faced with a dilemma. With the Abdication Crisis still fresh on the public's mind and war in Europe expected at any moment, the monarchy was in desperate need of an infusion of respect, romance and magic.

With an acute sense of imagery, the queen elected herself, at least in part, as the medium of projecting what was lacking. Not traditionally beautiful, she chose to play up her best features – her luminous skin, bright eyes and, yes, even her tendency toward matronliness – thanks to the magical dress designs of Norman Hartnell. All of these elements, combined with the liberal use of the many fabulous royal jewels at her disposal, helped the queen invent for herself the popular image of a romantic fairy queen that is famously exemplified in the series of portraits taken by Cecil Beaton in 1939. Even the stunning Liane de Pougy would have had a difficult time outdoing Queen Elizabeth The Queen Mother in those photos.

In this sense, the concept of queenly beauty is not simply reflective of the characteristics of a certain royal woman's face or body, but of her overall image and presentation. This is certainly true in the case of Josephine Bonaparte who is remembered as much for her refined beauty as for being the great love and consort of French Emperor Napoleon Bonaparte. While many of the contemporary portraits of Josephine certainly exemplify her fine features and apparent gentility, they do not necessarily reflect her as she really was, especially by the time she was fully vested in the public eye.

For one thing, there was the little matter of her teeth. Having been raised on a sugar plantation in Martinique, Josephine had early on been exposed to too much sugar and not enough dental hygiene. In short, her teeth were blackened from decay and her gums were swollen from irritation. Granted, dental health was not the priority it is today, so the expectations would not have been as high, but Josephine herself made it a point to conceal her teeth whenever and however possible. Her teeth aside, while most contemporary accounts of Josephine before she was married to Napoleon credit her with being merely pretty, they frequently point to her "sweet personality" as her best feature.

These days, a reference to a woman having anything remotely similar to "a good personality" has become something of "dating-speak" for "she's not very pretty, but she's awfully nice." In reality, the combination in a woman of a charming or magnetic personality and even moderate good looks often makes her appear far more attractive than a woman who is considered outright beautiful. For some legendary royal women, including Josephine, the legacy of their beauty is perhaps more directly a reference to this unique combination than to dramatically good looks.

Cleopatra is an excellent example of this phenomenon. Popularly perceived to be a beautiful seductress – and always portrayed as such – modern archeological finds have indicated that she was far from looking the way she was portrayed by Elizabeth Taylor in the prime of her life. An article in the January 2002 issue of *Harper's Bazaar* succinctly described Cleopatra as she was portrayed in contemporary images as "an ordinary-looking woman, short, with bad teeth and a bony nose." And yet, a 2004 list of the top 100 most beautiful women of all time, as compiled by Evian, listed Cleopatra at number 86 – above Rita Hayworth, among others. Now I know Rita Hayworth didn't have bad teeth and a bony nose.

So why do we still perceive Cleopatra as beautiful? Although I believe the complete answer is far more complicated, I personally boil it down to the basic idea that it is not only far easier to believe that a beautiful Queen Cleopatra seduced two great men and attempted to defeat the Roman Empire, but also much more romantic. That we can't seem to fully attribute her conquests of men and land to exceptional intelligence, acute political acumen and exceptional self-promotion – all of which should be incredibly attractive to any personally secure and politically powerful man – is almost embarrassingly indicative of our concept that queenly virtue is largely, if not fully, comprised of her superficial image. It's for this reason, in my opinion, that people want to believe that Josephine and Cleopatra were unsurpassingly beautiful, just as it's why many people still insist that the Duchess of Windsor wasn't attractive enough to "catch a king," so must have used little known sexual techniques and domination to trap him.

At the end of the day, it's the truly smart women who have grasped this concept. Among the best royal women in history are the ones who realized that it's not enough to be just beautiful or just smart, and it certainly doesn't do to be unprepossessing. When you boil it all down, few royal women have been as acutely aware of this as Queen Elizabeth I of England. Her prowess in this regard was remarkable and requires little introduction to anyone who is even remotely familiar with royal or political history. Though hardly beautiful and with her sex an obvious disadvantage, she managed to create a powerful image of herself as a magnificent and iconic figure who met every expectation of a woman and queen (despite being the "Virgin Queen") and fulfilled expertly the role of a man and king. Elizabeth's example is even more profound when compared to her half-sister, Queen Mary I of England, who, with neither the looks nor the understanding of the importance of image, failed miserably as queen. Perhaps Oscar Wilde was right when he wrote in "The Picture of Dorian Gray" that beauty "has its divine right of sovereignty. It makes princes of those who have it."

But while the overall beauty factor – which is perhaps more accurately an issue of image – seems to have made or broken a great many royal women, we are still left with the age-old "Chicken and Egg" question of which came first – a preponderance of beautiful royal women or the expectation that royal women should be beautiful? Given the dearth of contemporary images and descriptions – not to mention the sometimes questionable accuracy of both – of distantly historical royal women, it's almost impossible to qualify their beauty.

In the odd instance where we have anything approaching tangible evidence, it is usually incredibly limited or vague. For example, while there seems to be a plethora of contemporary accounts of the celebrated beauty of Eleanor of Aquitaine, wife of two kings, there is a definite lack of any accurate contemporary depiction of her, or even a detailed description of important physical features like eye color.

Even if we did have access to such intelligence, we would still be all too apt to base our opinions on modern standards of beauty. After all, it's a mistake made all too often with the portraits and photographs that are available to us. A biographer can write all day of the beauty and elegance of a queen who lived 400 years ago, but one look at a painting of the same queen can easily convince modern sensibilities of the opposite. And everyone knows that pictures can be incredibly deceiving.

Few people will disagree that Britain's Queen Alexandra, consort of Edward VII, was a beautiful woman in both her youth and middle age – a fact exemplified by both contemporary accounts and images. Even fewer people would fail to be amazed at how incredibly youthful she looks in photos taken of her in middle age. But even a cursory look at an un-retouched photo of the Queen in her late 50s – such as one included in Leslie Field's book "The Queen's Jewels" – is enough to convince anyone that the laws of gravity did indeed apply to Alexandra.

This brings me to my final point, although I haven't quite decided whether it's a notch on the side of the "chicken" or of the "egg." In either case, the story of queenly beauty would not be complete without the recognition that royal women have traditionally had far more chances than the average woman of actually being beautiful. And I don't necessarily mean genetics, as we're all aware of the historical dark side of genetics – or, more precisely, genetic inbreeding – on royalty. What I'm referring to has more to do with accessibility.

Like today, when the money that is so frequently the privilege of royal women allows the modern princess or queen to afford plastic surgery, royal women of the past also had access to the best science and technology had to offer. Cleopatra, it is said, took advantage of the bounty of the Dead Sea for the cosmetic benefits of the salt and mud. We know now that Queen Nefertiti had an early facelift, but we already believed that she used cosmetics and various other beauty treatments. Such treatments and applications would have been predominantly used by, if not only available to, royal women.

Money and privilege also brought royal women the luxuries and comforts that could keep them not only far healthier and, thus, better looking than their subjects, but also more elegantly coiffed and attired. And, at the end of the day, a beautiful woman whose features have grown haggard from disease, hard work and difficult living conditions, and who is wearing filthy rags and hasn't bathed in six months is likely to pale in comparison to a plain looking woman whose face is youthful and unmarred by scars or age, and who wears a dress of the finest cloth accented by beautiful jewels. Just like the picture of a 58-year-old-woman with access to photo retouching is going to look far better than that of a woman without it. Of course, I realize that there were plenty of exceptions to these simplistic examples, but there always are with general rules.

With all of this in mind, it perhaps comes as little surprise that so many of the historical royal women we know of today were renowned for their beauty and elegance, and those we have forgotten weren't. Accordingly, it's really no coincidence that modern royal women are trying desperately to keep up that tradition, so they, too, will be remembered as "beauty queens."

The Courting of Fat Mary

The royal marriage market has never been a particularly straightforward or painless institution. Still, a few historical cases of royal courting and marriage somehow manage to stand out as being particularly protracted and difficult. This was certainly the case with Princess Mary Adelaide of Cambridge, known both fondly and callously in her own time as "Fat Mary," whose prolonged and exasperating courting placed her for 14 years in something akin to a purgatory of the royal marriage market.

As a granddaughter of King George III and first cousin of Queen Victoria, Princess Mary was sufficiently royal to be at least considered by most foreign princes, but the distance between herself and the throne made her something of a consolation prize. Adding to her challenges were her lack of fortune – her Parliamentary allowance was just £3,000 a year – and her weight – even as a very young woman, she weighed around 210 pounds.

Right out of the gate, Princess Mary's prospects had seemed far from dim. In fact, one of her earliest suitors appeared around the time of her coming out in March of 1852. Although he was 13 years older than the 18-year-old Mary, Prince Henry (Hendrik) of the Netherlands was governor of Luxembourg and brother of King William III of the Netherlands, making him a more than respectable potential match for the young Princess.

However, after visiting England, ostensibly to inspect his potential bride, Prince Henry failed to make an offer. With little hesitation, he instead found his bride in Princess Amelia Maria da Gloria of Saxe-Weimar, whom he married in 1853.

If Princess Mary's journal entries accurately reflect her true feelings at the time, neither this initial rejection nor her marital prospects in general concerned her in the least. In truth, she had little reason to be concerned at this point. Despite her large size and small fortune, she seemed to have an abundance of positive attributes that had the potential to more than offset these two drawbacks. One contemporary described the Princess at age 19 as: "strikingly handsome, and her beautiful hair and dark blue eyes were much admired; she was dignified and graceful in her movements, and a remarkably light dancer. Always bright and animated, her ready wit and keen sense of humour always kept us continually amused." Queen Victoria once wrote that Princess Mary was "beautiful, spiritual, well-educated and possesses an excellent heart" and was "stronger than most of the young ladies of her age."

On the other hand, opinions as to Princess Mary's personality faults were both prevalent and consistent. Unlike the more formal manner of Queen Victoria and her Court, Princess Mary was carefree and casual. Although this made Mary popular with the masses, it did not always rest well with the Queen, who at times felt that "Princess Mary's popularity seemed ostentatious and almost deliberately sought." Many in royal circles and polite society agreed with the Queen that Princess Mary had a "forward manner" and was "fearfully pleasure-seeking." One story tells of how Princess Christian of Denmark, mother of the future Queen Alexandra, said of Princess Mary:

"[Her] conversation 'was not fit for young girls,' and she had seen her 'flirt to that degree that she had said to Alix [Princess Alexandra of Denmark] "If you ever become such a coquette as Mary you would get a box on the ears."'"

Nonetheless, while Mary enjoyed herself during her second London season in 1853, plans were afoot to ally her with another foreign prince. That year, Napoleon III of France suggested a match between Princess Mary and his cousin, Prince Jerome Napoleon, known as "Plon-Plon." The 31-year-old Prince was the son of Napoleon I's youngest brother, Jerome, the ex-King of Westphalia. And although he was at that time heir-presumptive to the French throne, like his father, Plon-Plon did not have the best of reputations. Prince Albert called him "the greatest scamp in all France" who "even *disgusted* the French." Most critically to Princess Mary and the British Royal Family, Plon-Plon was Catholic.

It perhaps goes without saying that Queen Victoria and Prince Albert did not like the idea of the match, but Prince Albert still felt it was necessary to broach the proposal with Princess Mary's mother, the Duchess of Cambridge, who was also strongly adverse to the idea. When Mary caught wind of the situation, she made no secret of the fact that she was utterly opposed to marriage with not only a Catholic, but "a man of character so notoriously bad that she herself was aware of it." When the official rejection of Plon-Plon's proposal was made, religion was given as the reason, but while this was the most polite course for refusing the match, it was in no way an empty excuse as Princess Mary was truly devout in her Protestant faith.

Amusingly, according to a newspaper account in 1857 – several years after the fact – Mary's "rejection" of Plon-Plon had caused "sore damage... to the heart of the corpulent wooer," who was described as a "poor, broken spirited suitor, whose state of depression has been beheld with compassion for some time past." Unlikely as it seems that Plon-Plon was truly a broken-hearted swain, he had certainly "recovered" from the rejection enough by 1859 to marry Princess Clotilde of Savoy.

Despite the elimination of Plon-Plon as a suitor, the French Imperial couple did not give up on their hopes of arranging a match for Princess Mary that would ally them to the British Royal Family, even if it was only in a distant way. In April 1856, the Empress Eugénie suggested the 22-year-old Princess Mary as a possible wife for Prince Oscar of Sweden. The Prince was marginally related to the Imperial couple through his grandmother, Désirée Clary, who was at one time engaged to Napoleon Bonaparte and whose sister had been the wife of Joseph Bonaparte. Only a few years older than Mary, Prince Oscar seemed a viable enough candidate for Queen Victoria to suggest a meeting.

As early as May 1856, at least one American newspaper had already caught wind of the situation, proclaiming: "Prince Oscar of Sweden is expected immediately to England, on a flirtation trip, to woo the hand of Princess Mary of Cambridge." The article described Mary as "young and beautiful." By that summer, the Prince was in England, where he duly met Princess Mary, but left without proposing. According to one account:

"He went on to Paris where apparently he informed Eugénie that he was disinclined to marry Princess Mary. No reason for his refusal was ever given but he was possibly put off by her rather casual manner… and also her vast size. If he were concerned to have a family this could have been a very real consideration for it was then believed that fat women had difficulties in childbirth."

An Unusual Journey Through Royal History

The Prince married Princess Sophie of Nassau the following year and in 1872 he became King Oscar II of Sweden. Although a sympathetic biographer of Mary assured the world that "while the Princess enjoyed his society, she never contemplated an alliance with the heir-presumptive to the Swedish throne," the fact remained that it was a high profile rejection, and quite possibly a key turning point in the courting of Princess Mary.

By this point in Mary's romantic life, she had at least three potential suitors, none of whom had come anywhere close to displaying a genuine interest in the Princess herself. This changed with the appearance of Victor Emmanuel of Savoy, King of Piedmont, Savoy and Sardinia, even if he was probably not the knight in shining armor that Princess Mary might have imagined.

Although he is most succinctly described as "A strikingly ugly man... [whose] camp manners and broad humor amused Paris and shocked London...", perhaps the most vivid description of Victor Emmanuel paints a picture of:

"...a squat man with enormously strong, thick legs and an immense moustache which swept up towards his little grey eyes in a ferociously intimidating crescent. Untidy in his dress and blunt in his speech, he was coarse in his habits. Detesting official banquets, through which he would sit glaring about him, his eyes rolling alarmingly, his hand on his sword, he preferred to eat huge peasant dishes of steaming ragout smothered in garlic and hot onions. His appetite for women was equally voracious and uninhibited."

In November 1855, the King made a state visit to London, and Mary had the opportunity to visit and dine with him several times. She even sat next to him during at least one meal, but he was supposedly on his best behavior, so she probably never saw him behave in a "voracious and uninhibited" way. Following his departure, she mildly commented that he was "naturally very shy, which he conceals under a brusque manner." She continued, "He is also far from prepossessing in appearance, but remarkably soldier-like, frank, and, I believe, clever."

Prior to meeting Victor Emmanuel, Mary had made a significant impression on the Italian sculptor Baron Carlo Marochetti when she sat for him in London. Nine months later, it was Marochetti who was empowered to make an offer of marriage on behalf of the King. Victor Emmanuel's first wife, Adelaide of Austria, had died in January of 1855. Since he already had several children by her, including three surviving sons, it's unlikely he was proposing out of a sense of dynastic necessity. It would have certainly crossed his mid, however, that an alliance with Britain would bring with it many advantages.

Queen Victoria sanctioned the proposal, but left the decision to Princess Mary, whose refusal of the Catholic King on religious grounds was "immediate." In a letter to Queen Victoria in September 1856, the Duke of Cambridge called his sister's reasons for refusing Victor Emmanuel's proposal "excellent and weighty." He elaborated:

"Princess Mary fully appreciates the many excellent and noble qualities of the King. She does not doubt that in him individually she would be happy, and she thinks, that the alliance would be popular in England; but Her Royal Highness feels that as the Protestant Queen of Sardinia she must be in a false position, and that a wife can never find herself thus placed without injury to her husband."

Queen Victoria responded to the Duke that his letter was "admirably written, and does dear Mary the greatest credit; she puts it on the *right* ground, viz. that of the *Protestant feeling* which should always actuate our family and to this we *now must* keep." More importantly, she continued, "It *effectually closes*, however, the door to *all Catholic* proposals – whether from Kings or Princes, which makes matters easier."

Victor Emmanuel went on to become the first king of a united Italy on February 18, 1861. In 1869, he made a morganatic marriage with his mistress, whom he created Countess of Mirafiori. Ironically, one of the King's daughters by his first marriage, Princess Clotilde, became the bride of Plon-Plon, Mary's earlier Catholic suitor, in 1859.

Contrary to Queen Victoria's statement that the elimination of Catholic suitors would make matters easier, the situation actually became more difficult – not to mention embarrassing – in January 1858, when Queen Victoria's eldest child, Princess Victoria, married Prince Frederick of Prussia. The fact that Princess Victoria was just 18, while Princess Mary was 25 was not lost on anyone in the Royal Family, who thereafter made it their mission to find a suitable husband for the elder princess.

Queen Victoria and Princess Victoria were particularly active on this front; so, not surprisingly, a great many of the candidates were German. At least two Prussian princes were suggested, including Prince Albert (Albrecht) and Prince George. Prince Albert, who was a cousin of Princess Victoria's new husband and several years younger than Mary, was deemed not only too young, but also "of the wrong temperament" for her. Prince George was suggested by Princess Victoria, but he made a morganatic marriage. Apparently, Princess Victoria also suggested the Archduke Leopold, although she disapproved of Augustus of Württemberg, despite the fact that he was reportedly "very fine-looking."

Several candidates came from the pool of eligible princes from the Saxon duchies. Among these, Maurice (Moritz) of Saxe-Altenburg, the son of George, Duke of Saxe-Altenburg, was a candidate when Mary was 28, but he married Princess Auguste of Saxe-Meiningen, who happened to be the sister of another of Mary's potential suitors, the Duke of Saxe-Meiningen. In retrospect, marriage to Maurice probably wouldn't have been a good thing for Mary since late 19th century gossip reported that the prince would "lie in bed weeks at a time merely because there was 'nothing worth getting up for'."

On the surface, another Saxon candidate, Gustave of Saxe-Weimar, seemed a good possibility. For one, he was a nephew of Queen Adelaide, consort of Britain's King William IV, on his mother's side. For another, he was the brother of Edward of Saxe-Weimar, who was a close friend of Princess Mary's brother, the Duke of Cambridge. Gustave also happened to be the brother of Amelia Maria, who had married one of Princess Mary's earlier suitors, Prince Henry of the Netherlands. But like so many other potential suitors, Gustave fell out of the running with no apparent explanation.

At least one set brothers was considered for Mary – Friedrich Franz II, Grand Duke of Mecklenburg-Schwerin, and his brother, William. History does not remember either one very fondly. One of Princess Mary's biographers described the Grand Duke as "a dreary widower," while his brother was even "less interesting." According to the same source:

"...the Grand Duke was dominated by his mother who only wished for a nice quiet princess whom she could control and was totally opposed to the idea of her son marrying the strong-minded and independent Princess Mary. The other

Mecklenburg prince was known to be wildly extravagant and had been refused by a number of princesses already."

Among the many candidates during this period, William VIII, Duke of Brunswick, was a front-runner as far as Queen Victoria was concerned. Despite the fact that he was said to be eccentric and unreliable, the Queen wrote in 1858: "The Duke of Brunswick is the match for her [Princess Mary] & I wish we could bring it about." It never was, however, and the Duke died unmarried in 1884.

The flow of potential candidates seemed unending, and additional possibilities included Prince Nicholas of Nassau, Prince William of Hesse-Philippsthal-Barchfield and Prince Waldemar of Holstein. The latter was dropped because he was "impoverished" and otherwise "unsuitable." At this point, Queen Sophie of the Netherlands improbably suggested the "dull" Prince William of Baden, even though she herself thought the match "would have been a case of 'fire and water'."

Throughout this period, Mary's attitude and resolve seemed to be constantly wavering. In 1856, when she was 23, she "showed no disposition to turn her thoughts in the direction of matrimony." But by November 1858, reality was clearly setting in. At that time, the 4th Earl of Clarendon – three time foreign secretary during the reign of Queen Victoria – wrote to his regular correspondent, the Duchess of Manchester, that Princess Mary "was reasonable about her not very brilliant prospects but she seems to think that marriage has become a necessity for her..." Less than a year later, on July 28, 1859, he wrote again to the Duchess, this time reporting that Mary told him "she had made up her mind to be a jolly old maid [which] I take the liberty of disbelieving."

Despite, or perhaps because of, the multitude of German candidates being considered, one thing Mary did seem to determine absolutely was that she was horrified of the idea of living at any of the small German courts. She even "stated categorically that she had no wish to leave her country." Perhaps it was as a potential alternative to such a "horror" that Mary and others in the Royal Family may have considered candidates from among the British aristocracy. According to one account:

"Among those whose names were passed about in society were the Dukes of Rutland and Newcastle, and Lords Canterbury and Hood, but the prospect of marriage with any of these was firmly rejected by Queen Victoria, who believed it would have been impossible for her to maintain her royal position."

Along these lines, a somewhat embarrassing situation occurred in 1860, when it is said that Princess Mary may have actually proposed to the 2nd Baron Skelmersdale. Unfortunately for Mary, Lord Skelmersdale was in love with Lady Alice Villiers, daughter of none other than Lord Clarendon. Never quiet on the subject of Princess Mary under normal circumstances, Lord Clarendon naturally felt inclined to refer to the incident in one of his many letters to the Duchess of Manchester. Around late June of 1860, he wrote that although he did not mention the situation between Mary and "Skelmy" to Queen Victoria herself, he had learned through a trusted source that the Queen "seemed quite aware that Mary's intentions *had been honorable* and that she must have been truly mortified." Lord Skelmersdale and Lady Alice married in August 1860 and went on to have nine children together. In 1880, he was created Earl of Lathom.

An Unusual Journey Through Royal History

Despite the fact that the pickings were becoming slimmer and slimmer, and Princess Mary was not – by 24, her weight was up to "at least 250 pounds" – the situation was not deemed so desperate in 1866 as to consider a match with Prince Albert of Monaco. The match was a primary ambition of the Prince's grandmother, Princess Caroline of Monaco, who had instituted the help of the Empress Eugénie to further her cause, which had several fundamental problems. Namely, that Princess Mary was 15 years older than the 17-year-old Prince Albert, the Prince was Catholic, and Queen Victoria maintained unhidden contempt for the legalized gambling that took place in the tiny principality. Personally undeterred, Prince Albert went on to marry twice, first to Lady Mary Victoria Hamilton, and second to Alice Heine, the widowed Duchess of Richelieu.

As luck would have it, Prince Albert of Monaco turned out to be Princess Mary's courting swan song. In March 1866, she finally met the man she would marry at a dinner party hosted by the Duchess of Cambridge. In her own succinct words, Mary described how the possibility of a lifetime of royal spinsterhood disappeared into oblivion:

"The wooing was but a short affair. Francis only arrived in England on the 6th of March, and we met for the first time on the 7th at St. James's. One month's acquaintance settled the question, and on the 6th of April he proposed in Kew Gardens and was accepted."

"Francis" was His Serene Highness Prince Francis of Teck, the product of the morganatic marriage of Duke Alexander of Württemberg and Claudine, Comtesse de Rhédy. Had his parents' marriage not been morganatic, Francis would have been heir-apparent to the throne of Württemberg. As it was, he was considered lesser royalty and was practically penniless. And although Mary had at one time indicated that she would prefer an older man (an idea Queen Victoria seconded), Francis was four years younger. On the plus side, he was considered very handsome and seemed in all other ways the ideal match for Princess Mary. According to Kinloch Cooke:

"Her future husband possessed the attributes that most appealed to Princess Mary. He was high principled, domesticated, a thorough soldier, and, above all, a strong Protestant. They had, besides, many tastes in common; he was endowed with much natural talent for music and also for drawing..."

Mary's brother, the Duke of Cambridge, wrote in April how "supremely happy" the couple appeared. He called Francis "a charming person" and said that Mary was "thoroughly satisfied at the resolution come to." So it was that on June 12, 1866, the courting of "Fat Mary" officially ended when, at age 32, she and Francis were married at Kew Church.

While Mary's weight may have been the most readily-applied reason for her long and bumpy road to the altar, it seems unfair to draw such a simplistic conclusion today. In retrospect, the reason may actually have been that Mary was so dichotomous; starting with the fact that she was corporeally unappealing due to her size, but also characteristically attractive.

Her appearance aside, suitors drawn by the allure of an advantageous match and an alliance with the British Crown often walked away baffled and turned off by Mary's personal strength and casual manner. Ironically, these were traits that made her immensely popular in her own country and would probably have done the same in almost any adopted country.

Finally, as important as making a good marriage was to Princess Mary and the British Royal Family, suitors who seemed bent on a marriage for purely political reasons, and were therefore quick to overlook Mary's drawbacks, were always strongly rebuffed. Similarly, dozens of candidates were flat out rejected as simply not being "right" for her, often for reasons that were ultimately overlooked in Prince Francis. Whether by accident or design, both of these scenarios reflect the love and respect the Royal Family – both collectively and as individuals – had for Princess Mary, regardless of her "faults."

In the end, despite all the years of frustration, embarrassment and disappointment, Princess Mary had managed to find not only a husband, but a husband with whom she was compatible and content, and who seemed to respect and appreciate her in return. Of course, the union also produced something no one could have ever foreseen – the couple's daughter, best known to Britain and the world as Queen Mary, consort of King George V.

Bugger Bognor... How's the Empire?

Britain's King George V, who triumphantly celebrated his Silver Jubilee only months earlier, lies in his bed at Sandringham House on the verge of death, surrounded by his family. Concerned with keeping his royal patient's spirits up, the king's physician reportedly suggests, "Your Majesty will soon be well enough to visit Bognor."

The King replies, "Bugger Bognor," and promptly dies.

Not exactly the ideal last words of a benevolent monarch, especially to the ears of the residents of Bognor Regis. So, naturally, *The London Times* duly reports that the late King's final words were, "How is the Empire?", thus ensuring that British subjects the world over believed that – even on his deathbed – the King's final concern was for the well-being of the British Empire.

Clearly, the business of royal last words is a difficult one. Being royalty, their final words are not only eagerly anticipated – often more so than those of other public figures – they're also held to a higher standard. While it's acceptable for the rest of us to say ridiculous things like, "I'm coming to play catch with you, Fido," or "Remember to water the plants," royalty are expected to make profound or significant statements, preferably regarding their successor or their earthly realms.

James V of Scotland did both when, as he lay dying in 1542, he uttered, "It came in with a lass and it will go with a lass." This thoughtful statement referred to the Stuart dynasty, which "came in" thanks to the marriage of Marjorie, daughter of Robert I of Scotland (Robert the Bruce), to Walter Stewart, 6th High Steward of Scotland. When the Bruce's only son, David II of Scotland, died childless in 1371, the throne passed to Marjorie and Walter Stewart's son, Robert II – the first Scottish king of the House of Stewart (Stuart). Thus, the second part of James' dying words was the realization that the House of Stuart would end with his another "lass," his 6-day-old daughter, Mary. Little did he know that Mary's son and heir, James VI, would not only perpetuate the House of Stuart in Scotland, but install it in England as well.

But such a resonant dying phrase is generally the exception, not the rule. Among my favorite royal last words are those that are either so mundane they are insightful or so ridiculous they are funny. Marie Antoinette, Queen of France, takes the cake (no pun intended) for her polite apology, "Monsieur, I ask your pardon. I did not do it on purpose," when, on ascending the scaffold, she accidentally stepped on her executioner's foot. For a woman who was considered vain and frivolous, this was certainly a very humble dying statement. On the side of the ridiculous is the Roman Emperor Gaius Caligula, who, after being stabbed repeatedly by his own Praetorian Guards, shouted in vain, "I am still alive!"

With so many dying words, it's no surprise to run across royals who've said the same thing at different times. Perhaps the best example of this is when an injured or dying person, in an attempt to appear brave, claims, "It is nothing." Both Henry IV of France in 1610 and Archduke Franz Ferdinand in 1914 said those exact words just before dying following assassination attempts.

Of course, royal history has passed down to us a plethora of pious dying words, especially from the days when only God and the Roman Catholic Church had authority over kings. When Charles V of France died in 1380, his final words were simply, "Ay Jesus." And, despite being known as "the Silent," William I, Prince of Orange, pleaded, "Oh my God, have mercy on my soul. Oh my God, have mercy upon this poor people," when he was assassinated in 1584.

Sometimes, however, these pious exclamations smack a bit of last-minute deal making with the great man upstairs, such as when the dying Charles VII of France asserted in 1461, "I hope never again to commit a mortal sin, not even a venial one, if I can help it." Too late.

Other royals are more concerned with the comfort of those around them. Britain's Merry Monarch, King Charles II, had been dying for such a long time in 1685 that his final thoughts were for the many courtiers and nobles who had attended him at his deathbed for so long. To his credit, he is reported to have said to them, "I have been a most unconscionable time dying, but I beg you to excuse it." Of course, it's also reported that his last words actually referred to Nell Gwynne, one of his many mistresses, when he entreated his brother and heir, The Duke of York, "Let not poor Nelly starve."

Which brings up the issues of multiple accounts and versions of a particular royal's last words. Anne Boleyn's last words, for example, are often said to have been, "The executioner is, I believe, very expert, and my neck is very slender." Those words, however, were actually spoken the day before the execution. Her *very* last words were, "Oh God, have pity on my soul."

Others spoke very few last words, but those few take an amazingly high proportion of variations. Versions of Napoleon Bonaparte's last words include: "France, the army, Josephine"; "Chief of the Army"; and, simply, "Josephine...". Similarly, Henry VIII said either, "Everything is gone - kingdom, body and soul!" or, "All is lost. Monks, monks, monks!" The bottom line here is that the numerous versions of a dying royals last words are often derived from the interpretations of the equally numerous individuals that so often surrounded them in their dying moments.

But even when the last words are confirmed, there are those that are all too often taken entirely out of context - especially historical context - and, as a result, exceedingly misunderstood. Consider Queen Victoria's dying words, "Oh, that peace may come." Contrary to what some might think, she was not referring to achieving the peace acquired only by death, but to the second Boer War, or South African War, which was in its final stages at the time of her death in January 1901.

It's nice to think that we will all manage to at least say something coherent when it's our time to say goodbye to this mortal world, but, as if dying weren't difficult enough already, a royal on the verge of death is expected to say something profound. Quite a responsibility, especially when you consider that an entire royal legacy can be overshadowed with the "wrong" last words.

All of this leads right back to poor George V on his death bed. Another account of his dying words makes "Bugger Bognor" sound positively philosophical. It seems that, after receiving a shot of morphine, the King's very last words were,

"God damn you." I wonder what *The London Times* would have made of that?

An Unusual Journey through Royal History
Volume II
by
Victoria Martínez

DEDICATION

To my parents, Jim and Grace Van Orden, for their never-ending love and support.

Foreword

My first impression of Tori is one I'll never forget. It was early 2004 and I was looking at ways to expand the website I had created, which at that time was called "The Unofficial Royal Family Pages" (now "Unofficial Royalty"). One of the ideas I had was to find a team of columnists who would write regular columns/editorials about royalty. So I posted a message on the site asking if anyone would be interested to contribute. My hopes for finding people were small, as I had nothing much to offer these authors in return, as the website was and is not-for-profit. All I could offer was an email address and an opportunity to publish stories on the Internet as part of a very popular website.

Tori was the first one to respond with a very enthusiastic email. Have you ever seen the DVD/Blue-Ray of the movie Shrek? The DVD menu consists of all the characters grouped together, and "Donkey" jumping up and down shouting "Pick Me!". That is a great analogy of the email that Tori sent me. How could I refuse? She also sent me a great sample of her work, which made me even more willing and happy to take her on. I haven't regretted it a single moment. Little did I know then that Tori would turn out to be the greatest success of the site. Her columns and stories always had an excellent viewing rate and were very popular among the visitors of the website.

Since then I've had the pleasure of meeting Tori and her husband David twice: once in Chicago, where they lived at that time, and another time in my home country, The Netherlands. I have come to known them both as genuinely nice people and I'm proud to count them among my friends.

After writing weekly columns for almost three years Tori let me know that other priorities meant that she had to stop writing for the site on a regular basis. Up until her first eBook was published her columns were a substantial part of the website and were still read frequently. Now I'm proud to let the visitors of Unofficial Royalty know that Tori's columns have been published and that the first eBook was such a success that another compilation of the columns that were once part of the site are now available in her second eBook. Enjoy the stories compiled in this volume. You will learn things about royal families from past and present that you may not have known before.

Thank you, Tori, for being part of the success of Unofficial Royalty, and for asking me to write this Foreword. Wishing you all the best for the future, and I'm already looking forward to your future publications!

Geraldine Voost, Founding owner of http://www.unofficialroyalty.com

Victoria Martínez

Praise for Victoria Martínez

"In her third collection of articles, Tori Martínez again turns her lively style and humour to royal topics, bringing many obscure facts to her readers' attention with her usual erudite irreverence. She rescues Bohemia's real King Wenceslas from his Christmas Carol and set him in the context of his nation's monarchy, and introduces us to several worldly Württemberg princes from more recent centuries, known for their great girth and fascination with the hospitality trade.

"But, as often, it is in writing about women's lives that Tori particularly excels, and this collection throws new light on the obscure Anne Hyde, mother of two Queens of England, and on numerous Princesses of Wales, all of whom, the author reminds us, had lives at least as dramatic as those of Diana. The classically beautiful French Empress Eugenie, best known for Winterhalter's stunning portrait, emerges as some kind of Single White Female, when it is revealed that she had an obsession with her forebear, Marie Antoinette, even to the extent of copying that luckless Queen's favourite colour.

"From Princess Margaret to George III's cloistered offspring, a plethora of royal ladies and other royal topics emerge form these pages in new lights, to entertain Tori's regular readers and introduce her to new ones."

An Unusual Journey Through Royal History

Janet Ashton, author of "The German Woman" and co-author of "The Grand Dukes"

More Praise

"In An Unusual Journey through Royal History, Victoria Martínez provides an interesting, fascinating look at the complex lives of a galaxy of remarkable royal figures. Filled with insight, wit, and sympathy, she offers an intriguing glimpse of many lesser-known figures in history in a captivating narrative that spans the middle ages to the modern era."

Greg King, author of *The Duchess of Windsor: The Uncommon Life of Wallis Simpson*

Tori Martínez does it again! Her witty forays into royal history always inform and charm, but the astonishing thing is how she finds these little historical tidbits. In her second volume of royal oddities, she gives breezy accounts of Bridal Customs, Princess Ka'iulani, Anne Hyde and even an impeccable rendering of the history of Good King Wenceslas. And, as in the first book, she does it with humor and above all sympathy.

I was especially struck by her chapter on Princess Margaret. New facts, as we know, have emerged about the attitude of the Royal Family and the government toward a marriage to Group Captain Townsend, and Tori does an excellent job not only of telling the old story but also giving the new facts that have materialized. She does so with intelligence and compassion for her subject. My favorite is the first chapter about the rather revolting Württembergs; some of them were definitely train wrecks, but they make for amusing reading.

Beautifully written and thoroughly researched, Tori's second volume of *An Unusual Journey Through Royal History* is a must-read for not only royal enthusiasts, but also for those who like the obscure, the absurd, and follies of the high-born.

Ilana D. Miller, author of *THE FOUR GRACES: Queen Victoria's Hessian Granddaughters*

ACKNOWLEDGEMENTS

I wouldn't be writing this if I had not had the support of so many people, both known and unknown to me, who helped make the first volume of *An Unusual Journey Through Royal History* a success.

To friends, family and mentors, as well as the many readers and reviewers who've bought, read and commented on the first volume – but whom I've never met – I owe a huge debt of gratitude. Without you, there would not be a "Volume II." I particularly want to thank my friends and fellow authors Ilana Miller and Janet Ashton, who are always there to read and comment on everything I write. Likewise, I am tremendously grateful to Hugo Vickers and Greg King, both authors whom I have admired from afar for many years and am now proud to count as mentors, informal editors and friends.

As with the first volume, I must also thank Geraldine Voost, who gave me my first opportunity to widely publish my writing on historical royalty on her fantastic Unofficial Royalty website. Most of the chapters in both volumes of *An Unusual Journey Through Royal History* originally appeared on that site. Similarly, special thanks to Ted Rosvall of *Royalty Digest Quarterly*, who has also given my writing a home and who originally published one of the chapters in this book.

Naturally, I want to thank with all my heart Jen Talty and Bob Mayer at Who Dares Wins Publishing. I couldn't be luckier to have to such great people to guide and support me.

Victoria Martínez

Introduction

When I published the first volume of *An Unusual Journey Through Royal History* in April 2011, I never anticipated publishing a second volume. Like all first-time authors, I was unsure of how my first book would be received. I had hoped, of course, that I would reach readers interested in history and/or royalty, but I also really wanted it to be a book that would help "convert" people without a particular interest in either subject. More than anything, I wanted to share with others that history doesn't have to be boring or sensationalized to be interesting.

As sales and reviews came in, I couldn't have been more thrilled with the response. Just as I had hoped, even people with little or no previous interest in royalty or history were reading and actually *enjoying* the book! Whenever possible, I talked to readers to find out what they liked most or felt was lacking in the book. More often than not, the response to the latter question was that most people wanted to read about a greater diversity of European royals.

Since I had only included in the first volume a portion of the articles I've written on European royalty over the years, I went through my files and realized I had left out significant articles about royals in places like Württemberg and Hawaii, as well as others that included everyone from the early 11th century King Cnut of Denmark to "The Great Heroic King Sihanouk" of Cambodia in the 20th century. From there, a second volume of

An Unusual Journey Through Royal History was born, thanks to readers of volume one!

As in volume one, the majority of the chapters in this book are comprised of articles written originally for the Unofficial Royalty website. One, "The Crown of Saint Wenceslas," first appeared in *Royalty Digest Quarterly*. All have been updated and revised for this collection and will – once again – make you think again about history and the royals who have dominated it.

Victoria Martínez

THE LARGER-THAN-LIFE WÜRTTEMBERGS

The minor ruling families of European royal history are often largely overlooked by modern royal watchers, who perhaps feel that these seemingly insignificant duchies, principalities and kingdoms just didn't have the imposing and provocative personalities that made up the larger and more prominent royal families. Although often true, there are also plenty of notable exceptions.

Among these, the Württembergs undoubtedly had more than their fair share of individuals who left larger-than-life impressions, despite a smaller-than-most position among Europe's ruling families. The many children and descendents of Duke Frederick II Eugene of Württemberg (r. 1795-1797) particularly stand out, some for their physical characteristics and others for their less corporeal legacies.

Occasionally, the chasm between these two categories was quite wide. For instance, in the former category was one of Duke Frederick's sons, Alexander, who was perhaps best known for his gross lack of redeeming physical qualities. In addition to having a "huge tumor" on his forehead" and "something brutish in his face,"[1] he was also obese – and with good reason. One story relates how, the morning after his wedding, Alexander's

---

[1] Ponsonby, D.A. The Lost Duchess. London: Chapman & Hall, 1958, p. 27.

new wife awoke "horror-stricken" to see "her husband beside her gnawing a big ham-bone with brutish ferocity."[2]

On the contrary, among the latter category were two highly respected – and eminently respectable – women. The first of these was one of Duke Frederick's daughters, Sophia Dorothea, who married Tsar Paul I of Russia (r. 1796-1801) and was, incidentally, exceptionally tall for her time. The second was, of course, Britain's Queen Mary, who was the descendent of a morganatic marriage between a grandson of Duke Frederick and a Hungarian countess.

Others made their mark purely by diverse associations and fateful positioning, such as with two more of Duke Frederick's grandsons. The first of these, William, Count of Württemberg (b. 1810), was the product of another morganatic marriage. But despite his low royal rank, William managed to make two relatively good marriages. He first married Theodelinda de Beauharnais, granddaughter of Empress Josephine of France, in 1841. The couple had four daughters before Theodelinda died in 1857. Secondly, in 1863, he married the sister of Prince Charles III of Monaco, Princess Florestine, with whom he had two sons. William was eventually granted the somewhat more distinguished title of HSH Duke of Urach in 1867, but he died just two years later and was succeeded in his titles by his eldest son.

In the early 20th century, William's sons very nearly had a golden opportunity when, as descendants of a Monegasque princess, nothing but a tissue-thin layer of direct heirs separated them from the crown of Monaco. But it was a situation that caused no small amount of consternation in France, where the idea of a German becoming a reigning prince of Monaco was

---

[2] Ibid

simply too much to bear. The prospect was prevented in 1918 by a provision in the new treaty between Monaco and France that limited the Monegasque succession to only Monegasque or French subjects.

Yet another grandson of Duke Frederick, Paul Wilhelm (b. 1797), made his impression on history almost entirely through his own adventures – specifically, his seven trips to the United States for the purpose of scientific exploration. His accounts of the American frontier remain his legacy to this day, while two of his unique associations historically intertwined him with one of the most elusive and captivating female figures in early American history – Sacagawea. A Native American woman of the Shoshone tribe, Sacagawea was the wife of Toussaint Charbonneau, who served as Meriwether Lewis and William Clark's French interpreter during their historic journey through the lands President Thomas Jefferson had acquired through the Louisiana Purchase. Pregnant when the journey began, Sacagawea had proved to be an invaluable asset, and her knowledge undoubtedly helped avert disaster on at least two occasions. She also bore her son, Jean Baptiste, on the epic journey.

During Paul Wilhelm's first journey through the United States between 1822 and 1824, he hired Toussaint Charbonneau as his interpreter, and then met 18-year-old Jean Baptiste Charbonneau at a trading post in Kansas. Paul Wilhelm was "greatly taken" with Sacagawea's son, and invited him to return to Germany with him in 1824.[3] There, Jean Baptiste had "five years of education in Europe"[4] before eventually returning to

---

[3] Württemberg, Paul Wilhem, Duke of. *Travels in North America, 1822-1824.* Ed. Savoie Lottinville. Trans. W. Robert Nitske. Norman, OK: University of Oklahoma Press, 1973, p.xx.
[4] Ibid, 271*n*

the United States, where he "became a guide for visiting royalty and traders."[5]

None of Duke Frederick's descendents managed to so deftly combine expansive physical proportions with more political contributions to Württemberg than his eldest child, another Frederick, who succeeded his father as reigning duke in 1797. Just prior to his succession, the younger Frederick had made a very good second marriage to Britain's Princess Royal, Princess Charlotte – daughter of King George III and Queen Charlotte. Despite this marital alliance to Britain, Frederick entered into a far more politically expedient association with Britain's great enemy, Napoleon Bonaparte. In return for certain favors granted by Frederick, Napoleon elevated Württemberg, which had become an electorate in 1803, to a kingdom in 1806. The grateful Frederick promptly married his daughter, Catherine, to Napoleon's youngest brother, Jerome, who was actually still technically married to another woman, at least in the eyes of the Roman Catholic Church.

King Frederick's grand new status was quite proportionate, shall we say, to his girth. For his obesity, he achieved the nickname "The Great Belly-Gerent," and Napoleon himself said something along the lines of "God had created the Prince to demonstrate the utmost extent to which human skin could be stretched without bursting." [6] Exaggeration perhaps, but Frederick was at least large enough to have "a piece cut out of the whist table at home to accommodate his stomach."[7] As for

---

[5] Karttunen, Frances. Between Worlds: Interpreters, Guides, and Survivors. New Brunswick, NJ: Rutgers University Press, 1994, p. 38.
[6] Van Der Kiste, John. The Georgian Princesses. Stroud, Gloucestershire: Sutton Publishing, 2002, p. 130.
[7] Fraser, Flora. Princesses: The Six Daughters of George III. New York: Anchor Books, 2006, p 180.

his wife, the British Princess Royal, although she had been called in her youth "uncommonly handsome" thanks to her attractive figure,[8] she too had become so large during her time in Württemberg that at age 50 she was virtually immobile.[9]

Not surprisingly, The Great Belly-Gerent's son, who succeeded as King William I in 1816, had a hard time filling his father's big shadow, although *his* son and successor, Charles I (r. 1864-1891), managed to do so in at least one respect – he was "...not only exceedingly stout, but also remarkably gross in his tastes, as well as familiar throughout the kingdom for his gluttony."[10] Fortunately, the last king of Württemberg, William II (r. 1891-1918), and his small family, left the world with an altogether more favorable impression of the ruling house.

Like so many of his predecessors, William II also liked good food, only in a far more professional context. In 1892, royal gossip extraordinaire, the Marquis de Fontenoy, raved:

"The King of Wurtemberg is the first restaurateur of his kingdom! He owns a café as well as the two most important restaurants in Stuttgart. One of the restaurants is called the Marcquardt, and is situated right opposite the Royal Palace, while the other and the café bear the name of Riesig, and are located under the arcades of the Koenigsbau."[11]

In fact, the King was not only a restaurateur, but also an hotelier, as the Marcquardt (or Marquardt) and the Riesig (or Reissig) were also hotels. In 1915, the Marquise further reported that "these two establishments have been a source of considerable revenue to the civil list, and still continue to prove

---

[8] Ibid, 87
[9] Ibid, 333
[10] Fontenoy, Marquise de (The). Revelation of High Life in European Palaces. Philadelphia: Hubbard Publishing Co., 1892, p 443.
[11] Ibid

of considerable profit to the private exchequer of King William..."[12] More specifically, in 1898, the revenue from the two hotels was estimated to be the equivalent of $50,000 a year,[13] while 10 years later it was said to be about the same.[14] Not bad, although considering that the King's annual civil list payment was $450,000 in 1891[15] and $490,000 in 1914,[16] the income from the hotels might not have been quite as big a supplement as the Marquise reported.

In any case, William did not place himself on a pedestal, and was called "one of the most simple-minded, anti-monarchical monarchs in Europe," who was "careless whether he is recognized as the King, only seeking to be friendly and affable to all."[17] This opinion would seem to be confirmed by a story circulating in 1898 about how an unsuspecting soldier hitched a ride to his Ludwigsburg barracks, only to find the guard at the barracks gate present arms to the kind soul who gave him a ride – none other than King William himself.[18]

King William II's knack of going incognito took an amusing twist in the next generation, and left history with just one more unique memory of the larger-than-life Württembergs. In March 1907, *The Washington Post* reported an account of a masked ball that had just been given at the United States Embassy in Berlin. Among all the expensive and intricate costumes, one was dubbed "the sensation of the ball." Described

---

[12] "Palace at Stuttgart Only Royal Abode Hurt in War." *The Washington Post*, 26 June 1915.
[13] "Royal Hotel Keepers." *Denton Journal* (MD), 3 Dec 1898.
[14] "Emperor Owns a Factory That Brings Him $50,000 a Year." *Daily Kennebec Journal* (ME), 28 Jan 1908.
[15] Fontenoy, 452
[16] "The Cost of Royalty." *Fort Wayne Journal-Gazette* (IN), 30 Nov 1914.
[17] Fontenoy, 446-7
[18] "His Royal Driver." *The North Adams Transcript* (MA), 15 Mar 1898.

as "a typical second-class Berlin cab driver" who carried a whip, had a "bulbous and suspiciously red" nose, and "clumsy and uncouth manners," this individual appears to have deceived everyone as he danced the night away with the elegant female guests and palled around with the gentlemen. At the moment of unmasking, the cab driver removed his costume, revealing himself as "a rotund, smiling, pretty peasant woman of the well-to-do farming class." That is, until the guests realized that the peasant woman had a further revelation to make. She was, in fact, Pauline, Princess of Wied, the only child of King William II.[19]

---

[19] "Prank of a King's Daughter." *The Washington Post*, 10 Mar 1907.

An Unusual Journey Through Royal History

Secondhand Queens

Only a handful of women in history have had the distinction of becoming queen twice.

Eleanor of Aquitaine is perhaps the first such historical queen who comes to mind. On July 22, 1137, at barely 15 years of age but already Duchess of Aquitaine in her own right, she married the 17-year-old heir to the French throne. One month later, her father-in-law died and her husband became King Louis VII. For almost 15 years, Eleanor reigned as Queen Consort in France, bearing her husband two daughters and even going on Crusade with him. But the marriage was not successful and the couple managed to have the marriage annulled on the grounds of consanguinity in 1152. With barely the blink of an eye, Eleanor seized her window of opportunity and six weeks after her marriage to the King of France ended, she married Henry Plantagenet – the future Henry II of England – and by 1154 was Queen Consort once again.

Another variation of the two-time queen is the woman who is queen both by marriage and in her own right. Two significant examples of this type are, coincidentally, the royal cousins Mary I of England and Mary, Queen of Scots. The Scottish Mary became Queen of Scotland in her own right at a mere six days old in 1542. In 1558, she married the French dauphin who became King Francois II of France a little over a year later. Unfortunately for Mary, her reign as Queen Consort in France lasted less than two years and, though her reign as Queen of Scotland lasted nearly 25 years, it was – as we well know – far from successful.

Nor did the Queen of Scots' cousin, Mary of England, fare much better. By the time she ascended to the throne of England in 1553, Mary was 37, unmarried and quite unattractive – not exactly an ideal position for any woman of the time, never mind a queen in need of an heir. But her one advantage – her kingdom – likely did wonders in securing a marriage for her with Spain's Prince Philip, himself heir to the Spanish throne. And, naturally, when he became King of Spain in 1556, Mary herself became his Queen Consort, although she never actually stepped foot in Spain. Mary was not destined to hold onto her foreign crown for long – she died less than two years later in 1558.

These three women – and others like them – certainly made their marks in history, but, becoming queen twice in two different kingdoms is one thing – becoming queen twice in the *same* kingdom is another matter entirely. In England and France, only two women have ever had that unique distinction – Emma of Normandy in England and Anne of Brittany in France. Secondhand queens they might have been, but Emma of Normandy and Anne of Brittany were no mere castoffs. Both women left a strong and lasting impression on their respective kingdoms, both politically and personally. But their lives were not all glitter and gold, filled as they were with violence, danger and political intrigue. The fact that both women managed to effectively navigate the dangerous waters of their time is a testament to their lives.

Born in Normandy between 982 and 986 to Richard I, Duke of Normandy, and his Danish wife Gunnora, there was little to portend that Emma was to become a pioneer among queens. But, in an age when foreign marriage alliances were still something of a rarity, her circumstances of birth would make both an ideal marriage pawn and prize. Her father was only the third Duke of Normandy, a title that had first been given to his grandfather, the Viking invader Rollo, who secured Normandy for himself and his heirs in 911. Naturally, with its strong Viking heritage, Normandy was a meeting place for Viking fleets bent on attacking England – a circumstance that was not lost on the King of England, Ethelred II the Unready. By the early 990s, England had successfully fought off one of the biggest Viking invasions in 100 years, but was facing continued Viking aggression nonetheless and was in desperate need of some relief. Ethelred thus turned to Emma's brother, Richard II – now Duke of Normandy – to arrange a diplomatic marriage to Emma and cut off at least one line of attack.

In 1002, without a modicum of free will, Emma sailed to England where she married Ethelred and made her home in Winchester. As she was a very young woman – possibly 18 or so – and in a foreign land, things couldn't have been easy for her. In addition to having to learn the Anglo-Saxon language, she also had to fulfill her most important role as queen consort – that of producing an heir. Nevertheless, it seems that she did both very effectively. By 1004, Emma had borne her husband two male heirs, Alfred and Edward, had taken an Anglo-Saxon name and was consequently on her way to becoming an important and powerful figure in her adopted country. All during an age when the role of queen consort was only just beginning to gain respectability and importance and in spite of the fact that her husband was not only ineffective as a ruler, but also took his frustrations out – often violently – on her.

But even with her growing personal power, Emma could do nothing to defend England from foreign invasions. In 1013 the country was overcome by the Danes under Sweyn Forkbeard. Ethelred, Emma and their children were forced to flee to safety in Normandy. Although Ethelred returned to England in 1014 and regained his throne, which he kept until his death in London on April 23, 1016, Emma and her children remained in Normandy under the protection of her brother. After the death of Ethelred, the struggle for power in England was fought between Ethelred's eldest son (by his first wife), Edmund Ironside, and Sweyn Forkbeard's son, the Danish Cnut (or Canute). By the end of 1016, the crown rested firmly with Cnut.

With all that was happening in England, Emma might have continued to stay in Normandy, where her safety was assured. Instead, she left her sons in Normandy and made her way back to England, where it is said she boldly proposed herself in marriage to King Cnut. According to some historians, Emma's writings seem to indicate that she was a Danish nationalist who wished to see England and Denmark joined, so it's quite possible that it was to this end that she proposed a marriage alliance with Cnut. Of course, it's equally possible, as many more historians suggest, that she was simply looking out for herself and her children. Either way, Cnut – like Ethelred before him – saw the value of an alliance with Emma, who brought both her Norman and English connections to the foreign king.

The couple was married in 1017, but not without their respective sacrifices. For Cnut, he first had to give up his mistress – the mother of his two illegitimate sons. As for Emma, she agreed that any children the couple had would be first in line to the English throne, effectively cutting out her children by

Ethelred, who remained in Normandy. It was a decision that would come back to haunt her; but, in the meantime, Emma produced a male heir for Cnut, Harthacanute, around 1018, and her personal power and influence seemed only to grow. Her position was further heightened, as through her husband's claims, she was also queen consort of Denmark and Norway. In her own right, she became a generous patron of many churches and monasteries, both in England and on the Continent, but her ultimate contributions to England were still yet to come. In 1035, King Cnut died and, with Harthacanute – his rightful heir – away in Denmark, Cnut's illegitimate son, Harold Harefoot, was chosen king of England instead.

Emma's sons by Ethelred finally returned to England in 1036, possibly to attempt to overthrow Harold. The attempt was unsuccessful and Emma's eldest son, Alfred, died after being captured, while Edward escaped to Normandy and Emma to Flanders. It was in 1040, during her exile in Flanders, that Emma did something no queen had ever done – she commissioned the *Encomium Emmae Reginae* – a written account of her life, the original of which is now in the British Library.

Finally, in 1040, the usurper Harold Harefoot died and Harthacanute became King of England. Without any children, the new king recalled his half-brother Edward back to England and named him as his heir. Emma also returned to England and continued living in Winchester, where she allegedly had an affair with her confessor – a bishop, no less. To prove the allegation false, Emma is said to have walked barefoot on nine red-hot plowshares – a test legend tells us she passed without a single burn. But a greater test was awaiting Emma. When Harthacanute died in 1042, Emma's eldest son, known as Edward the Confessor, became King of England. One of his first acts as king was to strip his mother of all her estates and valuables because, Anglo-Saxon chroniclers tell us, he felt that she had neglected him as a child.

Emma died in 1052, but she still had one more major contribution to make, even after death. While Edward the Confessor left no legitimate heirs to take the throne, Emma's grandnephew, William, Duke of Normandy, claimed that Edward promised him the throne in 1051. When the throne passed instead to Harold of Wessex and William took England by force in 1066, he used his relationship to Emma bolster his claim to the throne. Tenuous as that claim was, it certainly says something that he considered a relationship to a mere woman as proof of his connection to the English crown.

While Emma herself may have orchestrated her second marriage, Anne of Brittany was contractually bound to hers. As the sole heir to the French duchy of Brittany, Anne was an extremely valuable commodity on the marriage market, a position that was only heightened after her father's death in 1488 when she was only 11 years old. Before his death, her father had promised the French government that Anne would only marry with the consent of the French crown – a situation that virtually guaranteed a marriage that would enrich France. As a result, when Anne became Duchess in her own right, Austria, England and Spain – all fearing that France would seize the duchy and increase its continental power – sent armed forces to Anne's aid and a marriage by proxy was ultimately arranged to Holy Roman Emperor Maximilian I in 1490.

But this was not to be her first go around as a crowned head. Before the marriage could be consummated, King Charles VIII of France invaded Brittany in 1491 and forced Anne to annul the marriage to Maximilian and instead marry Charles himself, which she did on December 6th. Even with Brittany safely under French control, no chances were being taken. A law was created that ensured that if Charles died without an heir by Anne, she would be forced to marry the next in line to the throne. Almost as if by cruel fate, each of Anne and Charles' four children died in childhood and, when Charles died in 1498, the throne went to his cousin, who became Louis XII of France. Bound by the law created just for this purpose, Anne married Louis on January 8, 1499, after he divorced his first wife, Joan of France, for the purpose of keeping Brittany with the Crown.

If fate seemed cruel to Anne in marriage, it served her only slightly better in her other pursuits. Anne was incredibly fond of Brittany, which had secured from Charles VIII a guarantee of independence that had enabled Anne to administer the duchy – one of the richest in Europe – as its sovereign. By all accounts, she was a highly effective and intelligent duchess and spent her life guarding Brittany's autonomy from the French – an ambition that might have been fully realized had she produced more than one living male heir. If that had been the case, the French crown would have passed to the eldest son, and the Duchy of Brittany to the second. As it turned out, Anne and Louis had only two surviving daughters. By right, the eldest, Claudia, inherited Brittany on Anne's death in January 1514, but in May of that year, she married her cousin, Louis of Angoulême, who would become King Francis I of France the following year. As a result of the union, Brittany was finally blended with the French crown.

In addition to bringing Brittany to the crown, Anne left an indelible mark on French court life by introducing the concept of the queen's maids of honor. She was also a generous patron of the arts and even commissioned the *Book of Hours* – a collection of French manuscripts.

WHEN QUEENS TRUMP

Britain's Queen Elizabeth II, Denmark's Queen Margrethe II, and the Netherlands' Queen Beatrix. Three reigning female sovereigns – none of whom would be sitting on her throne today if she had had a brother.

But the times, they are a changing.

Since 1980, Sweden, the Netherlands, Norway, Belgium, Denmark and Luxembourg have all constitutionally recognized cognatic (or absolute) primogeniture, which dictates that the throne is passed to the eldest surviving child of the sovereign, regardless of gender. Thanks to these progressive countries and the impressive fertility of their respective royal families, there are currently no fewer than four European monarchies with an excellent chance of having a female sovereign within two generations – and not a single one of them need ever fear being upstaged by a brother.

In at least one case, however, a princess did upstage her brother. As the forerunner of the cognatic primogeniture movement, Sweden changed its constitution in 1980 and, instead of grandfathering the infant heir to the throne, Prince Carl Philip, his elder sister, Princess Victoria, took his place as first in line to the throne. Today, the very popular Crown Princess Victoria of Sweden is an example for her three younger counterparts in the Netherlands, Norway and Belgium, although they will come into their inheritance in a slightly more indirect fashion.

Just since 2001, Princess Elisabeth of Belgium, Princess Catharina-Amalia of the Netherlands, and Princess Ingrid Alexandra of Norway have all come into this world relatively assured of their futures as sovereign queens. The Netherlands was the first to follow Sweden's example, changing its constitution in 1983 – some 20 years before the birth of Princess Catharina-Amalia in December 2003. Norway followed in 1990, with the birth of Princess Ingrid Alexandra taking place in January 2004, while Belgium completed the quartet in 1991, although it was actually the first to celebrate the birth of a future queen when Princess Elisabeth arrived in October 2001.

But although the constitutions in their countries were changed well before their births, the change did not affect the positions of each of the princesses' fathers. In the cases of Princess Elisabeth and Princess Catharina-Amalia, their fathers are both first-born children, so have the right of succession in any case. In Norway, Princess Ingrid Alexandra's father, Crown Prince Haakon, might have been upstaged by his elder sister, Princess Märtha Louise, but an exception was made to ensure that he remained the heir.

It would have seemed that in Denmark, where Queen Margrethe II reigns, the laws of primogeniture would have been changed earlier rather than later than those of Sweden, Norway and Belgium. Instead, it wasn't until 2009 when the heir to the throne, Crown Prince Frederick, and his wife, Crown Princess Mary, had already provided the country with a male heir, Prince Christian (born in 2005), and a younger sister, Princess Isabella (born in 2007), that the Danish parliament voted in favor of cognatic primogeniture. As the eldest child of the Crown Prince and Princess, Prince Christian's place in line to the throne is unchanged. With the birth of twins – a girl and a boy – to the couple in 2011, however, the law ensures that Princess Isabella's position as fourth in line to the throne is not usurped by her baby brother Prince Vincent.

Spain began considering changing its laws of succession as early as April 2004, just before the wedding of Prince Felipe and Letizia Ortiz, with the effort led by Prime Minister Jose Luis Rodríguez Zapatero. As in Norway, a change to Spain's succession laws would not exclude Prince Felipe, but rather start with his heirs, making his eldest surviving child his heir. The rapid birth of two daughters to the Prince and Princess of Asturias seems to have made the change unnecessary, especially considering that a change in the law of succession in Spain requires nothing less than a constitutional amendment. For now, as long as the couple does not have a son, it would seem that a queen will one day inherit the Spanish throne.

This leaves us with Luxembourg, Liechtenstein, Monaco and – oh, yes – Britain. It seems a bit odd perhaps that Britain should be among this last group. After all, a queen regnant sits on the throne and the monarchy must feel pressure from its seemingly more progressive neighbors. On the other hand, Britain also has the advantage of three direct male heirs. Nevertheless, Queen Elizabeth has stated that she is agreeable to cognatic primogeniture and Britain has been playing with the idea of changing the laws of succession for a number of years. The latest bills were introduced in 1998 and 2004, but both times were withdrawn. In 2004, the Succession to the Crown Bill aimed not only to allow for equal succession, but also intended to repeal the Act of Settlement, which prohibits a member of the royal family who has married or become a Catholic from keeping their position in line to the throne, as well as the Royal Marriages Act of 1772, which requires that descendents of George II must have royal consent for marriage.

With two failed attempts in recent history and plenty of male heirs to the throne, it seemed unlikely that Britain would change the laws of succession any time soon, especially considering that such a change requires the approval of all 16 Commonwealth countries. And then, suddenly, it happened! Chalk it up to royal wedding fever and all hopes now being pinned on a new heir from Prince William and Catherine, The Duke and Duchess of Cambridge, but in late October 2011, the leaders of the Commonwealth unanimously approved a change in succession to cognatic primogeniture. The change applies immediately to the descendents of the Prince of Wales, which means that Princes William and Harry maintain their current places as second and third in line to the throne, respectively. But if William and Catherine's first-born child is a daughter, she will be next in line to the throne after her father even if she has a younger brother in the future. It also means that if William and Catherine do have a first-born daughter, the name of the child will be of tremendous importance as she will be a future queen. Which begs the question: could there be a future Queen Diana one day after all?

Unlike in Britain, where laws like the Act of Settlement and the Royal Marriages Act have historically been created to restrict succession, Monaco has been known over the years to make quite liberal amendments to the succession laws, primarily in an effort to ensure the future of the principality. When it became clear in the early 20th century that the heir to the Monegasque throne, Prince Louis, was not going to marry and produce an heir of his own, his father, Prince Albert I of Monaco, went to great pains to ensure the future of his dynasty. Prince Louis' illegitimate daughter, Charlotte Louise Juliette, was brought to Monaco and gradually legitimatized. A law was passed in 1911 to make Charlotte Prince Louis' acknowledged heir and a member of the royal family, but that law was later invalidated, so another attempt was made in 1918, this time allowing for the adoption of an heir to the throne. Under this new law, Prince Louis officially adopted Charlotte and, on May 16, 1919, she was created duchess of Valentinois and placed second in line to the throne after her father. Charlotte was married off to a suitable French count shortly thereafter and she eventually renounced her rights to the Monegasque crown in favor of her son – the man we remember today as the late Prince Rainier III of Monaco.

The failure of another Monegasque heir to marry and produce children caused the most recent changes to Monaco's succession laws. As Prince Rainier grew older and his health failed, it seemed apparent that his son, Prince Albert, was in no hurry to find a suitable wife and start a family. At that time, the laws of succession dictated that the throne could only pass to the direct descendents of the reigning prince. This meant that the moment Prince Albert ascended the throne; Princesses Caroline and Stephanie would automatically be excluded from the line of succession. At that point, Monaco would only be one step away – a childless Prince Albert – from an empty throne. So, in April 2002, the law was changed to ensure that in the event Prince Albert died – as sovereign prince – without a legitimate heir, the throne could pass to Princess Caroline or her legitimate heirs. The law also removed the adoption option instituted for Princess Charlotte in 1918. What it didn't do, however, was allow for cognatic primogeniture. Monaco still remains a principality that gives males take precedence over females in the line of succession.

Still, primogeniture is better than Semi-Salic Law – or that which leaves a woman to reign only as a last resort – which is still adhered to in Liechtenstein and – until recently – in Luxembourg. The Grand Duchy of Luxembourg owes its independent rule largely to its adherence to Semi-Salic Law. Beginning in 1815, the grand duchy was presided over by the Netherlands, whose king was also grand duke of Luxembourg. In 1867, Luxembourg officially became an independent country, although King William III of the Netherlands remained its grand duke. In 1884, King William's daughter, Princess Wilhelmina, became his heir in the absence of a son, and on the king's death in 1890; she succeeded her father as Queen Wilhelmina of the Netherlands. But with stricter rules of succession in Luxembourg, the grand ducal throne was passed to Adolph of Nassau-Weilburg, Duke of Nassau.

Ironically, within two generations of Adolph's reign as grand duke of Luxembourg, the grand duchy passed into female hands when his son and successor, Grand Duke William IV, produced six daughters and no sons. First to follow her father on the throne was Grand Duchess Marie-Adélaïde, who reigned from 1912 to 1919, followed by Grand Duchess Charlotte, who reigned until 1964. Since Charlotte's abdication, the grand duchy has been ruled again only by men, and the sisters remain the only two reigning grand duchesses of Luxembourg in history. As recently as mid-2011, it seemed that with plenty of male heirs in the line of succession, it was unlikely that there would be another reigning grand duchess any time soon.

That all changed on June 20, 2011, when Luxembourg became the most recent country to adopt cognatic primogeniture. As with Norway, the law has no immediate effect as the current heir to the throne, Hereditary Grand Duke Guillaume, is a first-born son. It does, however, make his younger sister, Princess Alexandra, third in line to the throne, and also means that women now have equal rights to the throne in yet another country.

Given that the Principality of Liechtenstein only granted women the right to vote in national elections in 1984, it perhaps seems obvious that it also still jealously adheres to Semi-Salic Law in regard to the line of succession to the throne. It may come as slightly more of a surprise to learn that the principality has never had a sovereign princess. Like Luxembourg, Liechtenstein has plenty of male heirs in sight, but unlike its counterpart, Liechtenstein shows no signs of changing the laws of succession. As a result, it seems highly improbable that there will be a sovereign princess of Liechtenstein any time soon.

Though it's not a European monarchy, any discussion of female succession would not be complete without mentioning Japan, which seemed at one time poised to remove the ban on female succession to the Chrysanthemum Throne given a dearth of male heirs. For a while it seemed that Princess Aiko of Japan – the only child of Crown Prince Naruhito and Crown Princess Masako – might be legally allowed to one day take her place as sovereign empress of Japan. With the birth of a son to the Crown Prince's younger brother in 2006, however, it seems that all efforts to change the laws of succession in Japan have been dropped. Princess Aiko now has little or no chance of becoming empress. Instead, her younger cousin, Prince Hisahito, takes her place as third in line to the imperial throne.

Indeed, all the royal succession changes in the past 30-plus years have been a major step forward for the countries involved and for the still incomplete women's movement around the world. And although there's a long way to go, a lot has been accomplished in a remarkably short period of time, especially when you consider the long road behind. In Norway, Princess Ingrid Alexandra stands to be the first sovereign queen in more than 600 years, while Crown Princess Victoria of Sweden will be the first in her country since Queen Christina abdicated in 1654. And in the relatively new kingdom of Belgium, Princess Elisabeth stands to be the first sovereign queen in its history.

Most importantly, public opinion in those countries that have changed their succession laws appears to indicate that the changes are widely accepted. Around the time of Princess Ingrid Alexandra's birth in January 2004, a Norwegian opinion poll found that only 20.7 percent of Norwegian men preferred the previous tradition of a male heir to the throne, while a mere four percent of Norwegian women felt the same. Not long after, another poll showed that popular approval of the monarchy had increased thanks to Princess Ingrid Alexandra's birth. Similarly, in the countries where changes are currently under consideration, such as Spain and Britain, the public appears to be largely in support of cognatic primogeniture.

Personally, I think that the only thing that could further improve upon having a Europe full of monarchies based on sexual equality for women would be further extending that equality to the men who marry the future queen regnants. After all, if a woman who marries a sovereign king becomes a queen consort, why shouldn't a man who marries a sovereign queen become a king consort? If sexual equality is the ultimate goal, then it must be the ultimate goal across the board.

In the meantime, I am one royal watcher who is looking forward to a future where queens finally trump.

An Unusual Journey Through Royal History

Royalty for a Day

It doesn't take a flood of royal weddings to remind us that almost every little girl dreams of someday being royalty for a day when she is married. From the tiara and white wedding dress to Wagner's "Bridal Chorus" and even the wedding bands themselves, newlyweds actually owe more than they know to royalty, who have been trendsetters in this regard for hundreds of years.

While the tiara is perhaps the object at a wedding most associated with royalty, it has actually been a common part of non-royal weddings since the 15th century. By that time, some form of a tiara was almost always included in an aristocratic woman's dowry and would undoubtedly be worn at her wedding. The concept trickled down to the lower classes and even in the early years of the tradition, women who couldn't afford a tiara of precious metal or stones would mimic the concept with flowers. Traditionally, tiara etiquette demands that a woman should not wear a tiara before her wedding day, as it is said to symbolize "the crowning of love."

Despite its longevity, the tiara's popularity among brides has waxed and waned dramatically over the centuries. It might have disappeared from the modern wedding ceremony altogether had it not been for the periodic high-profile royal wedding. Although Diana's use of the Spencer tiara for her marriage to Prince Charles in 1981 most immediately comes to mind, the ill-fated Princess Charlotte made an equally dramatic impact at her 1816 wedding when she wore a diamond tiara resembling rose buds and leaves, thus reawakening the trend among the aristocracy and gentry.

The idea of a white wedding dress is so engrained in our consciousness that it's easy to forget it has not always been a meaningful part of the marriage ceremony. Any bride worried that she does not have the right to wear white at her wedding will be interested in learning that the idea of white representing purity is a modern invention. It is actually blue that has traditionally represented purity, while white represented joy and happiness. This is the reason the Virgin Mary is always depicted in blue and brides in Biblical times wore blue dresses for their weddings.

According to bridal history, royalty not only introduced the white wedding dress, they also made it popular. Anne of Brittany is credited has having been the first bride to wear white when she married Louis XII of France in 1499. Considering that she had already been married to Charles VIII of France, with whom she had borne four children, her white dress certainly did not imply purity. Despite Anne's innovation, most women prior to the 19th century simply wore the best dress they could afford as a wedding dress, regardless of the color. By the time Queen Victoria came to the throne, most royal women wore silver wedding dresses – a tradition Victoria eschewed when she chose a white gown for her wedding to Prince Albert in 1840. This time the tradition stuck, enough so that a famous little wedding poem reads, "Married in white, you have chosen right."

Queen Victoria seems to have taken such sayings very seriously. In fact, she took the age-old saying, "Marry in the month of May, and you'll live to rue the day," so seriously that she supposedly banned her children from marrying during the month of May.

Like mother like daughter, Queen Victoria's eldest daughter, Victoria, The Princess Royal, was also an innovator when it came to weddings. A music lover, "Vicky" chose her own music for her 1858 wedding to Prince Frederick William of Prussia, including Richard Wagner's "Bridal Chorus," from the 1848 opera "Lohengrin," and Felix Mendelssohn's "Wedding March," written for Shakespeare's "A Midsummer Night's Dream." More recently, Diana's wedding certainly inspired at least a few brides to abandon Wagner in favor of Jeremiah Clarke's beautiful "Trumpet Voluntary" for their march down the aisle.

Although the modern British royal family traditionally exchanges wedding bands of Welsh gold, we supposedly owe the plain gold bands many couples opt for to Queen Mary I of England. She bucked the medieval and Renaissance trend of exchanging elaborate jewel-encrusted rings when she opted for a plain, simple wedding band for her marriage to Philip of Spain in 1554. And it's not just the wedding band that has been influenced by royalty. In 860, Pope Nicholas I decreed that a groom intending to marry must provide an engagement ring as a symbol of his intent. In simply following this edict, Holy Roman Emperor Maxmilian I may have been an accidental innovator when he gave Mary of Burgundy a diamond engagement ring in 1477. Even the humble ring pillow owes its origins to royalty, recalling in a humbler manner the method of carrying the crown during a royal coronation.

Undoubtedly, the most delicious and anticipated part of any wedding is the cake. Prior to the Restoration, however, it was more of a spectacle than a decadent treat. It seems the custom was for guests to bring small cakes, which were haphazardly stacked as high as possible. Bride and groom were then positioned on either side of the mountain of cakes and had to attempt to kiss each other without knocking the cakes down. If they were successful, it supposedly meant they would have a prosperous life together. Thankfully, during the reign of King Charles II, a French chef visiting London found the tradition so unbearable that he introduced the concept of a large, elegant and richly decorated cake – the forerunner of our modern wedding cakes. Tradition also tells us that a baker in London's Ludgate Hill modeled a wedding cake after the elegant spire of Wren's Saint Bride's Church in London, creating the first three-tier wedding cake.

Queen Victoria's wedding cake was reportedly nine feet in circumference, weighed 300 pounds and started the trend for cake toppers depicting the bride and groom. Her granddaughter, Princess Victoria Eugénie of Battenberg, had an even grander wedding cake when she married King Alfonso XIII of Spain in 1906. At more than six feet tall and weighing in at over 600 pounds, her cake had to be cut with a knife that was a foot and a half long. Perhaps more importantly, her grand confection introduced Spain to the tradition of the wedding cake for the first time.

Personally, my earliest image of a wedding outside of storybook fairytales was that of Lady Diana to Prince Charles. Of course, I know now that it was more of a fiction than the fairytales, but it certainly did a great deal to influence my concept of what kind of wedding I hoped to have when I grew up. A generation later, the marriage of Prince William to Catherine Middleton seems to have ensured that royalty has lost none of its influence on the ceremonies and traditions of marriage.

PRINCESS MARGARET: NEITHER LOVE NOR MONEY

In 2004, the legendary story of the young and beautiful Princess Margaret sacrificing her one-and-only true love in favor of loyalty to the Crown got a decided twist when classified files concerning the incident were released to the public. Prior to the release of these files, the account we were all accustomed to went something like this...

In 1955, barely 20 years since her uncle, King Edward VIII, decided that Wallis Simpson meant more to him than being king, Margaret was faced with an eerily similar choice: either marry the divorced war hero Group Captain Peter Townsend – 15 years her senior and a father of two – and lose her title, civil list payment and all rights as a member of the royal family, or don't marry him and keep her rights and stay in the good graces of the Church and Crown. Of course, we all know that she made the honorable, if not unromantic, decision to put duty before love.

Tragically, her life didn't seem better off for her decision. Her marriage five years later to Antony Armstrong-Jones was stormy and unhappy, and ultimately ended in divorce in 1978, making her the first royal to divorce since King Henry VIII. Apart from that, despite the jet set and glamorous lifestyle, the decadent holidays on Mustique, and the celebrity friends, she led what seemed like a largely empty and unhappy life.

As if all this wasn't bad enough, the file now available to the public in the National Archives tells us it didn't have to be that way. Unlike the Queen who, as head of the Church of England, was somewhat obliged to refuse permission for her sister's marriage to a divorcee, it seems the government had no opposition to Margaret's marriage to Townsend.

On the contrary, Prime Minister Anthony Eden led the development of a secret plan that would have allowed Margaret to marry her Prince Charming with almost no alteration to her existence. Under the terms of the plan, Margaret could have married Peter Townsend, kept her HRH title, her annual £15,000 civil list allowance (as well as the additional £9,000-a-year due she was entitled to upon marriage), and remained in England to carry out her public duties simply by renouncing her rights, and those of her descendants, to the succession. It was even implied in the file that Townsend might eventually receive an official allowance of his own. The plan went so far as to have speeches and letters announcing Margaret's decision to marry already prepared.

The file even indicates that the government was willing to change the law to make her marriage possible. The Lord Chancellor, Lord Kilmuir, was among those who believed that the Royal Marriages Act of 1772, which prohibited any descendant of George II to marry under the age of 25 without the monarch's permission, was outdated and an embarrassment that should be repealed. Reportedly, this sentiment was widespread enough that the Queen was asked if she would agree to its repeal. Despite being heavily censored, the file reveals that the Queen was at least prepared to reform the act to apply only to her children, grandchildren and those of the heir presumptive, which would leave Margaret free to marry without seeking the Queen's consent.

Not that repealing or changing the Royal Marriages Act would have made any technical difference to Margaret's cause. According to the file, the plan stated that Margaret needed only to wait until after her 25th birthday when she no longer needed the Queen's permission to marry. She could then go directly to the Privy Council and seek permission for her marriage, which, barring any unforeseen objections from parliament and the Commonwealth would be readily granted. In fact, it was only after her 25th birthday that Margaret announced she had decided not to marry Townsend.

So what of her reasons then? If the path was clear for her marriage to the man she loved, why didn't she seize her chance? Technically speaking, the only downside to the plan created by the government was that Margaret would have had to renounce her rights, and the rights of any children she might have, to the succession. But she must have known even then, as third in line to the throne after Prince Charles and Princess Anne, it was unlikely that either she or her future children would ever ascend to the throne, making it reasonable to assume her reasons were not dynastic.

Prior to the release of the file, I think it's safe to say that I was not alone in suspecting that perhaps Margaret had chosen the privileges of being a princess over love. In my mind, she had chosen material gain over happiness and had paid the price with an unhappy life. Now that we know that there was never any threat of losing her title, allowance and privileges, I am the first to recognize that this view was possibly unfounded and even – perhaps – unfair. Or was it?

After reading my thoughts on the subject, royal biographer Hugo Vickers wrote to me, "Anthony Eden's widow, the Countess of Avon, still alive, told me that the moment Princess

Margaret heard that the money might be cut off, she dropped any idea of marrying Townsend." This is to say that, before the plan was proposed by Eden that would allow her to keep her civil list income, when Princess Margaret believed she would be cut off after marrying Townsend, she gave up on the idea of marriage.

Officially, Princess Margaret's reason for not marrying Townsend was that "mindful of the church's teachings that Christian marriage is indissoluble" she could not marry the divorced Townsend. But at the risk of speaking ill of the deceased and without being judgmental, Margaret did not ever strike me as a "strict Christian," nor did many of her subsequent actions in life seem mindful of the doctrines of the church. That said, I recognize that her official reason was probably just that - *official*, but not the *real* reason.

At the end of the day, I think neither love nor money played a major role in her decision not to marry Peter Townsend. Ironically, I think it was a combination of loyalty and family pressure that caused her to choose as she did. Not loyalty to the crown, but loyalty to her sister (the fact that her sister was Queen was just incidental), who would have been put in a terrible position had Margaret chosen to marry Townsend. The family pressure, in my opinion, would have come from the Queen Mother, who still carried so much resentment for the Duke and Duchess of Windsor that the idea of seeing her daughter make the same choice would have been too much to handle.

So, in the end, not much has really changed. Princess Margaret still gave up the man she loved in favor of her family - who just happened to represent the Crown - and, officially at least, the Church. What *has* changed is the ferocity of my opinion of a woman who I once believed gave up what was most important to her simply to keep her tiara. In reality, I now believe that Margaret gave up her ticket to happiness for the greater happiness of her family and, quite possibly, the stability of the monarchy. And the money didn't hurt either.

It is perhaps not uncalled for at this point to briefly highlight two of the many ironies surrounding this incident.

Historically speaking, one of Margaret's primary champions, Anthony Eden, was, as Foreign Secretary in 1936, among those in the government who believed King Edward VIII should choose between abdicating the throne and marrying Wallis Simpson.

On the other side of history, we know that the queen did not repeal or even amend the Royal Marriages Act when she was asked to consider it in 1955, a decision that has greatly affected the course of her own son's life since the day he met his true love, Camilla Parker Bowles.

Victoria Martínez

The Crown of Saint Wenceslas

Little thought is generally given to the history of royalty in what is known today as the Czech Republic. Part of the problem is that the native Czech monarchy was commandeered by and merged into the Habsburg Monarchy in the 16th century, providing sufficient distance and distraction to effectively obscure the ancient kingdom from the casual observer.

Even the most recognizable elements of Czech royal history are not always recalled as particularly Czech. The name King Wenceslas, for instance, is probably more often directly associated with the English Christmas carol than with Saint Wenceslas, the Czech patron saint for whom the monarchy was named. But despite being the forgotten stepchild of monarchies, the history of the Crown of Saint Wenceslas is just as rich as any other European monarchy and certainly deserving of a closer look.

Shaping Princes and States

Well over a century before Charlemagne dominated his vast European empire, another Frank, King Samo, ruled over an empire of the first organized community of the Slavs from around the early 620s. Although the boundaries of Samo's empire are not fully known, the lands of Moravia and Bohemia –

both parts of the modern Czech Republic – were certainly part of it, with Bohemia at the center. But Samo was the glue that held his empire together and it dissolved after his death in 658.[20]

Following the demise of Samo's empire, political leadership in Moravia and Bohemia reverted to rule by chiefs of the various Slavic tribes, although a portion of Moravia did become a fief of Charlemagne's empire for a brief period.[21] By the 9th century, power began to re-consolidate, resulting in politically centralized rule in both Moravia and Bohemia.

Moravia was the first to claim a memorable sovereign – a Slavic tribal chief who came to power as Prince Mojmír I from about the early 830's.[22] Some 40 years later in Bohemia, a Czech chief of the Přemyslid dynasty pronounced himself Duke (or Prince, depending on the history book) Bořivoj I of Bohemia.

For a short time, Moravia and Bohemia lived peaceably side-by-side, with each making its early impressions on history. In Bohemia, as the first ruler of the House of Přemyslid, Bořivoj not only created the first royal Bohemian dynasty, but also gave the Czechs their name, as the Přemyslid chiefs had been members of the Čechové tribe, from which the word Czech is derived. [23] As for Moravia, its rulers helped introduce Christianity both in their own country and in neighboring Bohemia.[24]

Unfortunately for Bohemia, Prince Svatopluk of Moravia – a successor of Prince Mojmír I – had designs on more than just

---

[20] Gawdiak, Ihor, ed. Czechoslovakia: a country study/Federal Research Division, Library of Congress, 3rd ed. "First Political Units." Washington, D.C.: The Division, 1989. Available at http://lcweb2.loc.gov/frd/cs/cstoc.html, Accessed 30 Nov. 2005.
[21] Gawdiak, "Chapter 1: First Political Units."
[22] "Moravia." Encyclopedia Britannica 2002, Expanded Edition. DVD.
[23] Gawdiak, "Chapter 1: Bohemian Kingdom."
[24] Sayer, Derek. The Coasts of Bohemia: A Czech History. Princeton: Princeton University Press, 1998, p. 30.

the religious conversion of his neighbor. In scarcely 50 years, the rulers of Moravia had succeeded in creating a vast empire comprised of many of the lands of King Samo, including other parts of the modern day Czech Republic, as well as areas of Hungary, Poland and Slovakia.[25] Inevitably, Svatopluk also conquered Bohemia and absorbed it into what had become known as the Great Moravian Empire.[26]

The tables turned quickly back in Bohemia's favor after Svatopluk died in 894 defending his empire,[27] which lasted only slightly longer after his death than Samo's empire had after his, finally collapsing in 906.[28] In the aftermath, Bohemia, Hungary and Poland all clamored to claim the lands of the former empire and the three powers struggled for control until 1029, when Bohemia finally won control over Moravia[29] and took its place as the premier Czech power.[30] Moravia remained under Bohemian control for most of the next several centuries, although it was run as a separate margravate, usually under the control of a younger son of the Bohemian ruler.[31]

GOOD KING WENCESLAS

The newly Christian, post-Moravian Empire period of Bohemia's history produced one of the most recognizable Czech royals – Wenceslas I, Duke of Bohemia. His name in Czech was actually Václav and his legacy has little to do with the English

---

[25] Gawdiak, "Chapter 1: First Political Units."
[26] Ibid
[27] Maurice, C. Edmund. The Story of Bohemia from the Earliest Times to the Fall of National Independence in 1620. New York: G.P. Putnam's Sons, 1896, p. 20.
[28] "Moravia."
[29] "Moravia."
[30] Sayer, 30.
[31] Gawdiak, "Chapter 1: Bohemian Kingdom."

Christmas carol "Good King Wenceslas" that much later immortalized him.

Wenceslas came to the throne in 921 as the fourth Přemyslid ruler and a devout Christian. Just like Bohemia itself, Wenceslas' family was divided by religion. He and his father, Vratislav I, were both Christians, while his mother and younger brother were so-called heathens. By all accounts, Wenceslas was a genuinely good and pious ruler, both promoting and adhering to Christianity, while still tolerating the non-Christian beliefs and practices of his family.[32]

His brother, Boleslav, was not as forgiving, however, and murdered Wenceslas while he was attending a mass in either 929 or 935.[33] Boleslav succeeded his brother and initially tried to suppress Christianity through barbaric means,[34] but his actions created the opposite effect and Christianity ultimately came back stronger than before.

Wenceslas was interred at the church he established in Prague, Saint Vitus at Hradčany, where miracles were reported and credited to Wenceslas, leading to his beatification as a martyr.[35] So while Boleslav is remembered to history as Boleslav the Cruel, Wenceslas is revered as Saint Wenceslas, the primary patron saint of Bohemia.

A Kingdom Emerges

Residing beneath the shadow of the German-based Holy Roman Empire, it seems nothing short of a miracle that Bohemia

---

[32] Canning, John, ed. 100 Great Kings, Queens and Rulers of the World. New York: Taplinger Publishing Company, 1967, pps. 218-219.
[33] Sayer, 30.
[34] Maurice, 26.
[35] Canning, 221.

managed to maintain a semblance of autonomy, and even political and military power, for as long as it did. Not that Bohemia had escaped the notice of the German emperors, who requested – and usually received – tribute from generations of Bohemian rulers. Some had benefited from compliance, including Wenceslas I, whose "personal qualities" were so admired by Emperor Otto I that he was granted the title of King of Bohemia for his lifetime, although he refused to accept it.[36]

After Wenceslas' death, Otto changed his tact in regard to Bohemia, and in 950, the country became a fief of the Holy Roman Empire.[37] But membership had its benefits. Wars were won, profitable marriages were made and perhaps most significantly for the future, unmanageable and power hungry Czech aristocrats and competing royals were temporarily contained.[38] In addition, two more dukes were granted the title of King for their lifetime – Vratislav II in 1085, who ruled as King Vratislav I of Bohemia, and Vladislav II in 1158, who ruled as King Vladislav I of Bohemia.[39] But these were not hereditary titles and were only conferred by the reigning emperor in return for services to the empire.[40]

Finally, in 1198 Bohemia became a permanent kingdom under the rule of King Přemysl Otakar I.[41] With its elevated status, Bohemia gained new importance and, through a number of fortuitous circumstances, an increasing amount of power and autonomy. In 1212, Přemysl Otakar ensured the Přemyslid's hereditary right to the throne by securing a Golden Bull from the

---

[36] Maurice, 58.
[37] Gawdiak, "Chapter1: Bohemian Kingdom."
[38] Ibid
[39] Sayer, 31.
[40] Wandycz, Piotr S. The Price of Freedom: A History of East Central Europe from the Middle Ages to the Present. London: Routledge, 2001, p. 27.
[41] Sayer, 31.

Holy Roman Emperor that removed the imperial right to ratify Bohemian kings and formally confirmed the royal title and the succession in Bohemia.[42]

With the kingdom secured and powerful, Bohemia's position had advanced far enough that King Přemysl Otakar II was able to marry a German princess, Margaret of Babenberg – a marriage that added the dukedom of Austria to the Bohemian kingdom.[43] The marriage prospects were even better for Přemysl Otakar II's son, Wenceslas II, who married Judith of Habsburg, daughter of Holy Roman Emperor Rudolph I, in 1285. Things were really looking up for the Bohemian monarchy under Wenceslas II, who took control of Krakow and in 1300, became king of Poland.[44]

Undoubtedly, under the House of Přemyslid, Bohemia was "impressively unified by the standards of the time,"[45] but the good fortune of the dynasty disappeared under the reign of Wenceslas II's son, Wenceslas III. Already king of Hungary when he succeeded his father as king of Bohemia and Poland in 1305, within a year, Wenceslas III waived his right to the kingdom of Hungary, failed to successfully claim his right to the Polish throne, and was assassinated before he could produce a male heir for Bohemia.[46] Thus, a little over four centuries after it began, the reign of the House of Přemyslid in Bohemia was over.[47]

THE CZECH GOLDEN AGE

---

[42] Gawdiak, "Chapter 1: Growth."
[43] Ibid
[44] Maurice, p. 114-115.
[45] Sayer, 32.
[46] Naurice, 116-117.
[47] Sayer, 32.

With the death of Wenceslas III, the succession was up for grabs. Initially, the Holy Roman Emperor, Albert I of Habsburg, successfully lobbied for his son, who became King Rudolf I of Bohemia in 1306, but died in 1307. Next to the Bohemian throne was Henry, Duke of Carinthia, but he turned out to be an unpopular choice and was deposed in 1310.[48] His successor was John of Luxembourg, son of the Holy Roman Emperor. John was married to another daughter of Wenceslas II, Elizabeth of Přemyslid, which meant that the bloodline of the House of Přemyslid flowed through the veins of their son, one of Bohemia's greatest monarchs, Charles I.[49]

King of Bohemia from 1346, Charles was the first Bohemian monarch who was also a Holy Roman Emperor (Charles IV), a title he gained in 1355. He reigned in both roles until his death in 1378, during which time he did more to influence the Czech state than most rulers before or after him. Among his greatest achievements, he elevated the bishopric of Prague to an archbishopric and gave the archbishop the right to crown Czech kings, and he granted the kingdom autonomy by removing it as a fief of the Empire.[50] In his own time, Charles made Prague the heart of politics; education and architecture in central Europe; but even today, aspects of his legacy are still palpable. In 1348, for instance, he established the oldest European university, the Charles University of Prague[51].

Originally named Václav after St. Wenceslas (Václav I), Charles also placed special importance on anything associated

---

[48] Maurice, 117-118.
[49] Ibid, 118-119.
[50] Gawdiak, "Chapter 1: Golden Age."
[51] Roucek, Joseph S., ed. Central-Eastern Europe, Crucible of World Wars. New York: Prentice-Hall, Inc., 1946, p. 65-66.

with his namesake.[52] Even before becoming king, he initiated the construction of St. Vitus Cathedral on the site of St. Wenceslas' original church in Prague. At the center of the new cathedral, Charles had a special tomb and chapel made for St. Wenceslas.[53] For his coronation in 1347, he commissioned a crown that he dedicated to St. Wenceslas and which was used in subsequent Czech royal coronations. Today, the St. Wenceslas crown is kept near St. Vitus Cathedral inside Prague Castle, which Charles also rebuilt.

CHAOS

Following Charles' death, the pattern that had plagued previous generations of Czech royals – of a series of misfortunate reigns following a fortunate one – emerged once again when Wenceslas IV of Bohemia succeeded his father's glorious reigns in 1378, becoming both king of Bohemia and Holy Roman Emperor. Given that he acquired the dubious epithet "the drunkard," it comes as little surprise that Wenceslas was deposed as Emperor in 1400[54] and struggled through a turbulent reign as king of Bohemia until his death in 1419.

The throne then passed to Wenceslas' half-brother, Sigismund – the third Bohemian king/Holy Roman Emperor. Sigismund gained his imperial position in 1410 and, through his marriage to Mary, Queen of Hungary; he was also king of that country. When he died in 1437, the crowns of both Bohemia and Hungary went to his only child, Elizabeth, or, rather, to her husband, Albert II of Habsburg, Duke of Austria, thus ending the relatively brief Luxembourg dynasty in Bohemia. On paper,

---

[52] Sayer, 32.
[53] Ibid, 33.
[54] Maurice, 173.

Albert received a rich inheritance, but his reigns in both Bohemia and Hungary were plagued with revolts and infighting, and he died a broken man in Vienna in 1439.[55]

Disruption turned to chaos following Albert's death since his heir was as yet unborn. Born four months after his father's death, Ladislav Posthumous was king of Bohemia in name only, even after he was crowned in 1453. The real power behind the throne lay with a Bohemian noble named George of Podebrady, who served as regent.[56] Ladislav died prematurely in 1457, leaving behind no heirs, and Podebrady was elected king of Bohemia by the Czech nobility the following year.

For the Czechs, Podebrady was particularly attractive because he was a native Czech; but the choice inadvertently proved to be the death knell of native Czech leadership. The problem was that Podebrady was a heretic – specifically, a Hussite. Pope Paul II took exception to Podebrady's rule and in 1466, excommunicated the king and ordered a holy war against him. Eventually, Bohemia's neighboring rulers and even the Czech nobility united against Podebrady, although he successfully fought them all off until his death in 1471.

Disappearing Into History

After Podebrady, no appropriate Czech candidate could be found to replace him, making him the last native Czech ruler.[57] The closest the Czech nobility could get was Prince Vladislav of Jagellon, son of King Casimir IV of Poland and Elizabeth of Bohemia (Albert II of Habsburg's daughter). Known as King Vladislav II of Bohemia, he was succeeded in 1516 by his son,

---

[55] Ibid, 312-313.
[56] Sayer, 40.
[57] Ibid, 42-43.

An Unusual Journey Through Royal History

Ludvík (Louis). But the Jagellon dynasty didn't last long either, ending with Ludvik's death in 1526.

The Czech nobility went back to work and elected Archduke Ferdinand – brother of the Habsburg Holy Roman Emperor, Charles V – as king of Bohemia. Ferdinand had a tenuous tie to Bohemia through his marriage to Anne of Bohemia, the sister of the late King Ludvik of Bohemia, but he expressed little sentiment for the Czech national identity. Instead, he acted quickly to squash the independence and autonomy of Bohemia and make it the hereditary possession of the Habsburgs.[58] Ferdinand succeeded his brother as Holy Roman Emperor in 1556, by which time his actions had ensured that the fate of the crown of Bohemia would almost exactly mirror that of the Habsburg Monarchy right up to the birth of the Czechoslovak Republic in 1918.

The exception to this rule came in 1618 when the Protestant Czech nobility rebelled against the Habsburgs and, in 1619, offered the throne to Frederick V, Elector Palatine.[59] Frederick's advisors warned him against accepting the offer, but he did it anyway, possibly encouraged by his wife, Elizabeth Stuart, daughter of King James VI of Scotland and I of England, who supposedly said she would "rather eat sauerkraut as the wife of a king than roast meat as the wife of an Elector."[60] The couple duly took up residence in Prague, though their reign lasted just one year, earning them the epithet, "The Winter King and Queen."

The kingdom of Bohemia returned to the care of the Habsburg Empire to doubly disastrous effect. This time, the

---

[58] Ibid, 42.
[59] Ibid, 45.
[60] Akrigg, G.P.V. Jacobean Pageant: Or, the Court of King James I. Cambridge: Harvard University Press, 1962, p.335.

Czech lands suffered not only in terms of a permanent loss of political independence, but of almost complete suppression of cultural and religious identity.[61] After 300 years of this subjugation, it's not surprising the history of the Czech monarchy is largely glossed over as compared to other extinct monarchies. And though a short overview such as this hardly does full justice to a monarchy that thrived for nearly 800 years, it does open a window to the history of the Crown of Saint Wenceslas.

---

[61] Gawdiak, "Chapter 1: Historical Setting."

An Unusual Journey Through Royal History

ALMOST A QUEEN

More than 300 years before Lady Diana Spencer married Prince Charles, she was the last Englishwoman to marry an heir to the throne. As a mere "Lady" (just barely), she was also one of the then rare cases of a female commoner marrying a high-ranking royal. Pregnant before a legitimate marriage could take place, she went on to produce two future Queen Regnants. She secretly converted to Catholicism at a time in British history when to do so was akin to treason. In short, she led a more interesting life – and got away with a lot more – than some prominent British Queen Consorts; but, alas, Lady Anne Hyde, Duchess of York, never became Queen and, as a result, is frequently overlooked in the annals of history.

Although born into a good English family in 1637, Anne was essentially just the insignificant daughter of a lawyer who was slowly rising to prominence in an unstable Parliament. In 1641, Anne's Royalist father, Edward, became an unofficial advisor to King Charles I and, by the time of the Civil War, he had joined the King's Council as Chancellor of the Exchequer. But being a rising star in a turbulent King's precarious court was not exactly a great place to be. Disagreements with the King led to Edward Hyde being appointed as the guardian of the Prince of Wales – the future Charles II – and it was Edward who accompanied the Prince on his initial escape from the Civil War in 1646.

After Charles I's execution and the abolition of the monarchy in 1649, the Prince of Wales became – at least to Royalists – the exiled King Charles II. Around 1651, Edward Hyde became the new King's chief advisor and was ultimately appointed Lord Chancellor in 1658. This rise to power in exile would ultimately pay off in abundance when the monarchy was restored in 1660; but, in the meantime, Edward's family was already profiting from his advancing career. In 1654, Anne was appointed as Maid of Honour to Charles II's sister, Mary, Princess of Orange – a move that eventually put her in direct contact with the King's brother, James, Duke of York.

One thing led to another and, depending on which account you believe, James and Anne were either married or betrothed secretly in Breda on November 24, 1659. At the time, although James' position as Duke of York and heir presumptive was tenuous, the "alliance" was still technically and completely inappropriate, as Anne was not even the daughter of a peer. Everything would change dramatically, however, by the spring of 1660, when the monarchy was restored and the royal family returned to power. Having returned with the King to London, Edward Hyde sent for his family – including Anne – to rejoin him. Reunited with her lover/husband, Anne quickly informed James that she was pregnant.

Whether, in his newly confirmed position, the Duke liked it or not, he officially married Anne on September 3, 1660 in London, although the public announcement of the marriage was not made until December 21st. During the interim, Anne braved the anger and intrigues of almost everyone around her, including her previous mistress, the Princess of Orange, her new mother-in-law, Queen Henrietta Maria, and even her own father. When told of the marriage, Edward Hyde became furious at his daughter, going so far as suggesting to the King that Anne be immediately sent to the Tower of London, where she be placed under strict guard in the dungeon to await execution.

As if that wasn't bad enough, the Princess of Orange arrived in London and was immediately dead set against the marriage, on the basis that Anne was a commoner. Rather than just express anger over the match, the Princess also took affirmative action – hatching a plot designed to cast doubt in the Duke's mind as to his wife's virtue. She also, as a dutiful daughter, immediately notified her mother – the formidable Queen Henrietta Maria, now Queen Mother – who wrote a scathing letter to the Duke demanding to know why "he should have such low thoughts as to marry such a woman." More forebodingly for the marriage, the Queen Mother set sail for England to personally settle the matter. In direct opposition to everyone else, the King expressed his desire that the marriage be validated and made public. In the midst of all the chaos, Anne gave birth to a boy on October 22, 1660. But, as is often the case for the weary, Anne had no rest from the tumult.

With the Queen Mother due at Dover, the King set out to greet her, but not before making a gift of 20,000 pounds to Edward Hyde and leaving a signed warrant raising him to the peerage as Lord Hyde of Hindon. Meanwhile, the plot hatched by the Princess of Orange was having the desired effect, and probably would have worked if the Princess had not died unexpectedly, repenting her role in the plot on her deathbed and causing her co-conspirators to come clean. Finally, as the King was the King, he undoubtedly impressed his own will on his domineering mother, who eventually relented. With all the antagonistic parties at bay, Anne was finally officially recognized as the Duchess of York. As for Lord Hyde, he was further rewarded in 1661 when Charles made him the Earl of Clarendon.

Anne's victory over the strength of the Court not only secured her position, but also cemented her forceful personality and, ultimately, her power over her husband. Diarist Samuel Pepys said, "The Duke, in all things but his cod-piece, is led by the nose of his wife." Her domination of her husband, combined with an imperious attitude, didn't earn her much popularity at Court and she was often the subject of various rumors, accusations and intrigues. Insult was most certainly added to injury each time her husband embarked on yet another not-so-secret affair. But, with a libido surpassed only by the King, the Duke's "extracurricular" activities didn't seem to keep him away from his wife's bed. All told, in a little over a decade of marriage, the couple had eight children – four boys and four girls – although only two survived.

Despite her unpopularity at Court, Anne did manage to leave at lasting legacy outside of her contribution of two future Queen Regnants. Not a real beauty herself (Pepys called her "plain"), Anne seemed to appreciate beauty around her – that is, as long as it wasn't directly involved with her adulterous husband. Shortly after their marriage, the Duke and Duchess of York commissioned artist Peter Lely to paint a series of portraits of the most attractive women, both respectable and otherwise, at Charles II's Court. The portraits would be named for both for their subject and their home – Windsor Beauties.

Contradictory to the political mood of the time, the Duke and Duchess of York secretly converted to Catholicism in 1669. Anne wrote a document explaining her reasons for the conversion, which her husband published after he became king. In effect, the letter explains that, despite the fact that she would lose her friends and any respect due to her because of her action, she converted because it was the only thing she could do to save her soul. Apparently, others shared this belief, including the King, who converted to Catholicism on his deathbed. No matter what was done in secret or on deathbeds, Charles demanded that the couple's living children, Mary and Anne, were raised as Protestants – something that would come back to haunt the Duke in later years.

Around the time of the their conversion, it had become clear that the Queen, Catherine of Braganza, would not have any children. At this point, both the Duke and Duchess must have recognized that they and their children would ascend to the throne on the death of Charles. Near the end of 1669, however, any dreams of a family dynasty must have been severely battered when a fourth son, Edgar, was also the last son to die an early death. At the same time, another daughter, Henrietta, also died. Pregnant again by the summer of 1670, Anne fell ill, living long enough to see the birth of her fourth daughter, Catherine, on February 9, 1671. Catherine would also die young, but Anne would not live to know it – she died on March 31st, 1671.

Anne's early death precluded her not only from ever becoming Queen, but also from the flattering honors given to her successor, Mary of Modena. In 1683, for instance, Dutchess County, New York – one of the 12 original counties of that American state, was named for the second Duchess of York. Despite the odd spelling (explanations range from simple spelling mistake to the use of an earlier lexicon) it was an appropriate eponym considering that when England took control of the colony – previously known as New Netherlands – in the 1660s, Charles II renamed it in honor of his brother, the Duke of York.

On the other hand, Anne's death also kept her from the problems associated with her husband's troubled later life. As a converted Catholic herself, Anne would have undoubtedly played a similar role to that of Mary during James' largely disastrous reign and subsequent forced abdication. She would have also had to stand by and watch as her own daughters usurped her husband's throne in the name of the religion she so cherished. Instead, she was largely consigned to the back pages of history – almost a queen, but not quite.

The Monarchy Giveth, Taketh and, Sometimes, Disposeth

Royal gift giving used to be a simple matter. Back then, if you were a loyal subject come to pay your respects, a little gold and frankincense – maybe even some myrrh for that extra boost – would go a long way in putting you in the good graces of the king. For his part, all the king had to do was give away a few hectares of arable land to his lowlier vassals and perhaps throw in a coronet to sweeten the deal for his well heeled subjects.

But those were the good old days. These early years of the 21st century have capped off a long decline of the more "simple pleasures" of the royal gift giving tradition – on both sides of the throne. The culmination of this deterioration came – at least in Britain – in late 2002 when, it was alleged, members of Prince Charles' staff were discovered to be selling official royal gifts for profit. While the resulting inquiry report minimized most of the claims, the stigma of the accusation still remained, and new guidelines regarding official gifts were nonetheless put in place for all royal households in Britain.

So where did things go wrong?

To begin with, while royal gift giving has certainly always been a part of most monarchies, the rules (if there were any) were often vague, informal, and subject to change at any time. The reigning etiquette of royal gift giving was dependent on a number of circumstances, including the political and financial circumstances of the country, the background and preferences –

and even the ethics – of the monarch, and the mood and generosity of both the monarch and the subjects. Irregularity aside, there was usually a pretty darn good reason for the exchange of favors at court – demonstrating or gaining loyalty and support.

When William the Conqueror became King of England on Christmas Day in 1066, he wasted no time in confiscating lands and estates from the existing English nobles and replacing them with his faithful Norman and French allies, who would continue to owe William their allegiance and their swords in return. Under this system, William's favorites were safely in charge of half of England's land by the end of his reign. It's little wonder that he managed to keep the crown securely on his head for 21 tumultuous years.

On the Iberian Peninsula more than 400 years later, matters were not much different. With an intense desire to wrest Granada from the Moors, but few funds in the treasury to sufficiently finance the endeavor, the "Catholic Kings," Isabella and Ferdinand, had little choice but to offer the ruling classes the promise of their fair share of both the conquered lands and the booty in exchange for their financial and military support. As in the case of William the Conqueror, the strategy worked, and both parties benefited as a result.

But not all cases were so straightforward. Monarchs often had a nasty way of giving away generous grants of land, money, and titles in an act of seeming beneficence, just to take them back when it suited their will. Henry VIII proved to be the king of this very strategy, demonstrating that he could bring someone like Cardinal Wolsey to the height of wealth and power, just to take it all for himself when the cleric displeased him. Henry then proved himself equally crafty when he gained critical support for the dissolution of the monasteries by giving large tracts of the land he took from the church to important members of the nobility. Of course, not even the man who helped make the dissolution possible was safe from the temperamental monarch. When Thomas Cromwell (who himself profited in any number of ways thanks to the dissolution), also ran afoul of Henry, he, too, was charged with treason and executed. I suppose it's very easy to give away what you plan to take back by force in due time.

Fortunately, Henry didn't ruin it for everyone. The monarchy continued to give away everything from titles to generous grants of land to pensions to everyone from war heroes to court jesters to former mistresses in return for their allegiance, their service and their "favors" (not necessarily in that order). The high point in Britain seems to have been the Restoration – a time of extremely generous royal patronage. Charles II was giving land and titles away left and right, both to reward those faithful to him during the interregnum and to purchase new supporters. He was also a tremendous supporter of science and the arts. In return for his generosity, Charles seems to have had a lot of fun (especially with the ladies). He also kept his throne.

Throughout history, for the monarchs' loyal (aristocratic) subjects, royal gift giving often extended beyond continued loyalty and financial support to regular cow-towing and token generosity. Appearing regularly at court was expected. Regularly entertaining the monarch and his or her entourage to suitably high standards was expected. Kissing up was a good idea. And gifts of cloth of gold, precious stones, or cold hard cash at high holidays was greatly appreciated. If you were a common subject, repaying the monarch's favors might consist of blind loyalty if you were of little real use, or tolerating extended periods of royal non-payment for goods and services if you provided some sort of lowly service.

Things went on pretty much in this way for some time. The aristocracy got richer, the newly rich were ennobled, and the more humble subjects got the occasional commemorative memorabilia and royal grants of land for use by "the public." But somewhere along the way, things changed. All at once it became neither socially acceptable nor financially feasible for the monarchy to give away large gifts to select individuals, while the growing number of upwardly mobile loyal subjects found gift giving to be an innovative way of expressing physical gratitude (and possibly even ingratiating themselves, if the gift was generous enough) to the increasingly distant monarchy.

Today, royal gift giving consists more of what the subjects give the monarchy (and what the members of the monarchy do with those gifts) than on what the monarch gives his or her subjects. Sure, most monarchs still confer titles and honors to their subjects and occasionally make public land grants; but how many monarchs buy their subjects – in general – wedding and birthday gifts, and – in particular – everything from jewelry to food to pets?

So, given the improbability that any monarch is going to give his or her subjects individual gifts – not to mention make non-politically correct big ones to select individuals (at least publicly) – what do people expect to get in return for these royal gifts? Well, considering history, if either the person or the gift is humble, they can probably expect nothing but the sheer joy of giving. If the person and the gift are more generous, however, they might be the happy recipient of the honor of the royal presence, an invitation to the palace, or even official royal patronage. In the case of the latter, these individuals are more often than not wealthy foreign businessmen or officials with something to gain, as opposed to loyal subjects simply showing their respect or gratitude. For the former, however, there is innate folly in the act of giving a wealthy individual you don't know who already has everything he or she could possibly wish for something you think "they might like," no matter how outrageously expensive or adorably humble. It's like buying off the wedding registry for a couple you hardly know. Chances are, it's going to be either: a) returned/exchanged; b) "regifted"; or c) thrown in the trash.

And herein lies the heart of the trouble with modern royal gift giving. The royals have enough stuff. They don't need more. As generous as it may seem to give a gift, our ancestors probably had at least the basis of a better system – one where pledging your loyalty and support to one another was, literally, as good as gold.

Victoria Martínez

HAPPY PRINCESSES OF WALES: A ROYAL OXYMORON

"I often think that we can trace all the disasters of English history to the influence of Wales." –The fictional Dr. Fagan in Evelyn Waugh's 1928 novel, *Decline and Fall*.

While Dr. Fagan's statement was clearly intended as hyperbole, it certainly has an application within the context of the modern and historic British royal family. Although I risk sounding equally hyperbolic, many of the disasters in the lives of the women who became Princess of Wales can be traced to their elevated title and position.

When we hear the term "Princess of Wales," most of us tend to think immediately of Diana and the tragedy and sadness of her life, but the role carries with it a long legacy of tragedy and sadness going all the way back to Joan of Kent in 1361. In all, nine women have held the title of Princess of Wales, and many of their stories rival Diana's.

A quick memory jog reminds us of names like Katherine of Aragon – wife of Henry VIII, Caroline of Brunswick – wife of George IV, and Alexandra of Denmark – wife of Edward VII. Among these three Princesses of Wales, there was the first royal divorce, a miserably contentious marriage, and a notoriously unfaithful husband. Dig a little deeper into the history of the role and you also find a highly repressed wife and mother, an unwilling pawn in the royal game, a mother who hated her son, the wife of the most reviled English monarch of all time, and a lively woman broken by tragedy.

Surprisingly, while there have been only nine Princesses of Wales, the title of Prince of Wales has been conferred 21 times since the first English Prince of Wales, Edward of Caernarvon, was granted the title in 1301. Their history is not exactly a lucky one either, with six dying before they could accede to the throne and one forced to forfeit his rights. Of the 13 who did accede, eight either never married or married after becoming king, further contributing to the relative dearth of Princesses of Wales. As Edward of Caernarvon was among this latter group – he was already King Edward II when he married in 1308 – and the title of Prince of Wales skipped over his son, it would be 60 years until the first English Princess of Wales graced the pages of history.

The first Prince of Wales's grandson, Edward Plantagenet, the Black Prince, became the second Prince of Wales when he was invested in 1343 at the age of 12. The long awaited Princess of Wales arrived on October 10, 1361, when he married his cousin, Joan of Kent. It somehow seems appropriate that the first Princess of Wales in English history should have been problematic right from the start. Known as "The Fair Maid of Kent," Joan may have been famously beautiful, kind and lively, but she was far from being a "maid" when she married the Black Prince. In fact, she had already been married twice, with one husband still living.

At the age of 12, Joan secretly married Thomas Holland just before he went on crusade. During her husband's absence, Joan – who failed to confess the marriage – was forced to marry William Montague, a son of the Earl of Salisbury. On Holland's safe return to England several years later, he took the bizarre step of becoming steward of the Montague's household while he petitioned the Pope for an annulment of his employers' marriage. The plea was successful and Joan's marriage to Montague was pronounced bigamous and subsequently annulled, but not before Montague imprisoned Joan in her own home. In due course, she was returned to Thomas Holland, with whom she had five children before his death in 1361.

With barely a pause for breath, she married the Black Prince that same year at the age of 32. Not only were both directly descended from Edward I, they were only two years apart in age and had grown up together at the court of Edward III after the death of Joan's father made her a royal ward. By most accounts, the Black Prince had been in love with Joan for many years, so when he found her between husbands, he jumped at the chance to marry her, although his parents were known to be against the match. Even the Archbishop of Canterbury had warned him against the marriage since Joan's second husband, the Earl of Salisbury, was still alive. Despite it all, the couple somehow managed to obtain the assurance of absolution from the Pope and they were married forthwith.

While the marriage was reportedly happy, the circumstances of their lives were not. The first ten years of their marriage were spent fighting – and not always winning – fierce wars in Aquitaine, where the Black Prince was duke. During that time, they had two sons, but the eldest, Edward, died when he was just six. The family returned to England in 1371, right in time to experience the worst of the plague, which killed Joan's mother. During a final failed attempt to save Aquitaine, the Black Prince's health deteriorated and he died in 1376, missing his chance to be king of England by a little over a year. Instead, their eldest surviving son became the nine-year-old King Richard II on the death of Edward III in 1377.

As the mother of the new king, Joan had power and respect, but happiness continued to elude her with each new tragic event. She died, broken, in 1385, pleading with her son the King to spare the life of one of her sons by Holland, who had murdered a member of the royal court. Richard II granted the pardon, but Joan didn't live to know about it, dying the day before.

If Joan's life was surrounded by tragedy, the life of the next Princess of Wales would epitomize tragedy itself. Anne Neville became the second Princess of Wales on her marriage to Edward, Prince of Wales, son of Henry VI, in 1470. There is little doubt Anne was used as a pawn by her father, Richard Neville, the first Earl of Warwick, who will always be remembered as "The Kingmaker" during the Wars of the Roses. Whether or not she held any affection for her father or her new husband, it must certainly have been a blow when both were killed within a year of her marriage, leaving her an unprotected, fatherless widow during one of the most tumultuous periods of English royal history.

She wasn't a widow long before Richard, Duke of Gloucester, made his move. While the image of Shakespeare's evil hunchback wrenching the grieving Princess of Wales from her husband's grave to a miserable second marriage is almost certainly an exaggeration, Anne's life as the wife of Richard III could not have been considered a happy one. With chronic ill health, Anne stood by as her new husband stole the crown from his nephews and more than likely had them murdered. Her personal misfortunes reached a peak when her only son died suddenly in 1484 – less than a year after being created Prince of Wales – while she and Richard were away.

During her final illness, rumors abounded that Richard was planning to discard Anne and marry his niece, Elizabeth of York. Anne's subsequent death only fanned the flames and it was suggested that Richard poisoned her, although it's more likely that she died of tuberculosis. Although we will never know whether any of the rumors were true, they did much to contribute to Richard III's downfall and, perhaps fortunately for Anne, her death in March 1485 saved her from having to experience his ignominious death at the Battle of Bosworth on August 22, 1485.

It is almost as unnecessary to rehash the painful life of the next Princess of Wales as it is with Diana. That said, Katherine of Aragon's misfortunes more than withstand comparison with both her predecessors and her successors. Her marriage in 1501 to Arthur Tudor, Prince of Wales, and eldest son of Henry VII, made her a 16-year-old Princess of Wales. Less than five months later, she was the 17-year-old Dowager Princess of Wales. On the basis that Katherine claimed she and Arthur had never consummated their marriage, the Pope issued a special dispensation allowing her to become betrothed to the new Prince of Wales, Arthur's brother Henry.

Mostly due to the groom's young age, but with the added benefit of avoiding making the bride a Princess of Wales twice, the marriage didn't actually take place until after the groom acceded to the throne as Henry VIII in 1509. Although her husband was chronically unfaithful, the marriage was said to be a happy one. That is, until Katherine failed to produce a male heir. From here, the story needs little retelling; but, to sum up… Henry had his marriage to Katherine annulled – returning her former title of Dowager Princess of Wales, forced her into exile, illegitimated their daughter Mary and kept mother and daughter from seeing one another. Katherine was doomed to die alone in 1536, almost 150 years before the next Princess of Wales, Caroline of Ansbach, was born.

When Caroline married the son of the Elector of Hanover in 1705, she was an intelligent and relatively attractive minor German princess. Less than 10 years later, when her father-in-law became King George I, she took a major step up in royal life when she and her husband became the new Prince and Princess of Wales. Her new role carried even more importance than most Princesses of Wales because, as George I's ex-wife was imprisoned in Germany, Caroline was the first lady of the land. Unfortunately, therein lay just one of her many problems.

Beginning a tradition that would last all the way through the Georgian Age, George I and his son shared a deep mutual dislike for each other, were political opposites, and fought constantly. Relations between the two men were so bad that at one point one of the king's advisors suggested that the he get rid of the Prince of Wales for good by having him transported. Naturally, the spitefulness of the relationship spilled over to the Princess of Wales, who the king suspected of trying to steal his supporters on behalf of her husband. On another occasion, the king was misinformed that his son had challenged him to a duel and immediately put both the prince and princess under house arrest and took over the guardianship of their children. Needless to say, life was often difficult for Caroline under George I.

To further compound matters, despite the fact that the marriage was not unhappy and the couple respected each other and generally had good relations, Caroline still had to deal with her husband's constant infidelities. To her credit, she decided it was a losing battle and instead took the bull by the horns and began to personally select her husband's mistresses, making especially sure that they were not as pretty as she. In this and almost everything else, Caroline proved herself to be consistently smarter and stronger than her husband. When he finally became king in 1727, it was widely believed that George II was guided in all things by his wife. A well-known verse during his reign read:

"You may strut dapper George, but 'twill all be in vain,
We all know 'tis Queen Caroline, not you, that reign."

Unfortunately for Caroline, all was still not well. The curse of strained relations between father and son carried on between George II and his son and heir, Frederick, Prince of Wales. Separated from his parents when they left Hanover for London in 1714, he did not rejoin them until 1728 as a young man of 20. In this case, the prince actually didn't get along with either of his parents and, once again, life was miserable. Matters got worse when Frederick married the next Princess of Wales, Augusta of Saxe-Gotha in 1736. Although Caroline had the upper hand in selecting her new daughter-in-law, Augusta soon came under the control of her husband and, together, the couple did more to alienate themselves from the king and queen than Frederick ever did on his own.

At one point, Caroline called her son, "the greatest ass, and the greatest liar, and the greatest canaille [rabble], and the greatest beast, in the whole world, and I most heartily wish he was out of it." Sadly, Caroline died at the height of the troubles with her son, leaving Augusta in a position similar to hers as Princess of Wales – first lady of the land under the reign of her antagonistic father-in-law. Once again, life was difficult for the Princess of Wales – a situation that became tenuous when her husband died unexpectedly in 1751. With seven living children and an eighth on the way, Augusta logically took the only reasonable path available to her – she made her apologies to the king and did her utmost to repair the breach.

Her efforts were successful and she was granted full custody of her children and was even appointed Regent in the event that the king should die before his new heir reached his majority. Her life, however, was not a smooth and happy one. As Dowager Princess of Wales, she devoted herself to her children to the point of severe over protectiveness, eventually alienating herself from several of them. Having given birth to her ninth child four months after her husband's death, she then had to watch as most of her children lived unhappy or controversial lives. And, despite her official reconciliation with the king, relations between them remained strained and she felt mistreated and maligned. Her death saw her treated little better when, during her funeral procession, insults were shouted at her coffin.

Worse would be said of the next Princess of Wales. Much worse. Smelly, ugly, rude, indelicate, and adulterous are just a few of the "nicer" comments made about Caroline of Brunswick. Of course, life had not been made easy for Caroline when she arrived in England in 1795 to meet her betrothed – the future George IV – and was greeted by his mistress. Famously, when the Prince of Wales met his bride-to-be, he promptly left the room, said that he was not feeling well and ordered brandy. Not exactly an auspicious start to a marriage and, in fact, things went downhill from there. Inexplicably, the couple managed to conceive a child in what can only be described as an extremely drunken attempt by the prince to consummate the marriage.

Barely a year after the marriage began, the Prince of Wales was determined that it would end, and so began 26 years of marital hell for both himself and Caroline. The couple was effectively separated after 1797 and Caroline was only allowed to see her daughter under supervised visits. Over the years, Caroline's behavior, which had always been crude at best, was becoming increasingly outrageous, as well as embarrassing to the royal family. It was rumored that she had given birth to an illegitimate child and an official investigation was launched. Although she was found innocent of the charges, other unpleasant facts had arisen during the investigation and her reputation was forever sullied. Not that she did anything to make anyone think otherwise. Her outrageous behavior was carried with her on her travels to Europe, making her a laughingstock there as well as in Britain.

Real tragedy struck Caroline in 1817 when her daughter by the Prince of Wales, Princess Charlotte, died after giving birth to a stillborn son. With nothing left for her in Britain, Caroline continued her travels in Europe while her husband desperately, but unsuccessfully, tried to secure a divorce. When he ascended to the throne in 1820 as George IV, he had absolutely no intention of having Caroline crowned next to him. But just as he made every effort to keep her away, Caroline made an equally diligent effort to be crowned with her husband. On July 21, 1821, she made it all the way to the doors of Westminster Abbey, where she was publicly barred admission. Rejected, ill and broken, she died just a few weeks later, an uncrowned queen.

Much has been written about the next two Princesses of Wales and most of it has documented the trials and unhappiness of their lives. Theirs is a story of daughter-in-law succeeding mother-in-law as Princess of Wales, although almost no other similarities can be drawn between Alexandra of Denmark and Mary of Teck. While Alexandra was a renowned beauty who set the style for fashion and elegance at court, Mary wished only to please her husband's conservative and outmoded sense of fashion. On the other hand, while Mary brought quiet reserve and regality to her role as Princess of Wales, Alexandra's influence was much more ethereal. And while the two women did share a remarkable ability to remain publicly stoic and unruffled under the worst of circumstances, neither of them led what could be called terribly happy lives.

Beautiful she may have been, Alexandra could not keep her Prince of Wales, Bertie, from being consistently unfaithful to her throughout their marriage. Prone to deafness, Alexandra's hearing got progressively worse as she aged. When rheumatic fever followed the birth of her third child, she was left with a permanently problematic knee, which became known as the "Alexandra Limp". To add tragedy to misfortune, her eldest son died suddenly in 1892. As for her daughter-in-law, Mary, she, too, saw a son die early in life, then looked on as her husband died, her eldest son renounced his rights to the throne for a woman she found utterly objectionable, and two more sons predeceased her.

All told, each of these women led lives such that, had Diana known the full extent of them, she may not have been so fast to accept the role of the ninth Princess of Wales.

Victoria Martínez

THE EMPRESS WHO LONGED TO BE A QUEEN

Before Spanish aristocrat *Eugenia de Montijo* married Napoleon III, Emperor of the French, in January 1853, she had a good deal going for her. As Countess of Teba, she was titled in her own right. She was also rich, well connected, intelligent, generous and beautiful. But while her marriage further improved her fortunes by elevating her to astounding social heights as Empress Eugénie of France, her position was by no means popular or secure. To begin with, the Second French Empire was in its infancy, and although Louis-Napoleon had effectively transitioned from president of the Second Republic into Emperor Napoleon III, he was not a brilliant ruler. His choice of Eugénie as his wife was also widely considered to be less than brilliant given that mere aristocratic respectability and beauty were not viewed to be sufficient qualities for an empress – even for the Bonapartes.

Aware of the opposition and perhaps feeling nervous and unsure in her new role, it's not surprising that Eugénie chose to attach herself to an iconic royal woman after whom she could model herself. What is surprising is whom she chose for this critical role – none other than Queen Marie Antoinette.

Given the circumstances, it would probably have been more sensible for Eugénie to select as a model someone not so closely associated with excess, scandal and – worst of all – revolution. But such logic did not seem to apply to Eugénie, whose negative characteristics are recalled as frivolity, vanity, capriciousness and superficiality – all of which eerily echo those attributed to Marie Antoinette herself. To further confound the imagination, Eugénie was not only fascinated and obsessed with Marie Antoinette, but, in the words of author David Stacton, she even "fancied herself as a reincarnation" of the ill-fated queen.

As inappropriate and eccentric as Eugénie's sense of historical attachment may have been, she made no effort to hide it. Not long after her marriage, she publicly declared her affinity by appearing as a slightly modernized Marie Antoinette in a portrait by Winterhalter. Years later, she reaffirmed her dedication when she dressed as Marie Antoinette for a masked ball at the Tuileries Palace. In a way, it was like a triumphal return of the "new" Marie Antoinette to the place where the original Marie Antoinette and her family had been kept under house arrest during the French Revolution.

Ultimately, France's Second Empire was to be defined, at least in part, by Eugénie's desire to emulate Marie Antoinette and duplicate the Court of Louis XVI. Royal châteaux and palaces were dutifully furnished with Louis XVI furniture and decorated in modern interpretations of the Louis XVI style that eventually became known as "Louis XVI Imperatrice." Not surprisingly, the adaptive style soon became popular among the wealthy and the socially aspiring. Eugénie's Marie Antoinette-inspired retro-style also heavily influenced women's fashions. In an undoubted nod to the skirt-extending panniers of Marie Antoinette's day, Eugénie wholeheartedly embraced the cage crinoline in 1855, thus sparking a fashion craze. And just as Marie Antoinette's patronage of clothing designer Rose Bertin had helped make her a style icon of the 18th century, Eugénie depended on Charles Frederick Worth to do the same for her in the 19th century.

Not surprisingly, Eugénie easily attached herself to almost anything that had been of interest to or associated with Marie Antoinette. One such attachment was for the *Petit Trianon* – Marie Antoinette's personal paradise located in the grounds of Versailles. Likewise, although many of the royal jewels associated with Marie Antoinette had been lost or stolen during and after the French Revolution, Eugénie made good use of those she could get a hold of. Among these was the 140.5-carat Regent diamond, which Marie Antoinette had once jauntily worn in a large black velvet hat. For Eugénie, it became the centerpiece of two successive tiaras. Among her most cherished jewels must have been Marie Antoinette's pearls, which had come to Eugénie via the Queen's daughter, the Duchesse d'Angoulême.

No detail was too small for Eugénie, who went so far as to make Marie Antoinette's favorite color – Nattier blue – her own personal favorite, incorporating it whenever possible into her clothing and interior design. For her part, Eugénie's passion for the color is said to have inspired Tiffany & Co. to adopt it for their now-signature boxes. The Empress even out-Marie Antoinette-ed Marie Antoinette when she adopted the late Queen's custom of giving dolls dressed in contemporary Paris fashions as gifts, only with the improvement that Eugénie's dolls were made to resemble her.

Many similar comparisons can be drawn between Eugénie and Marie Antoinette, but deeper parallels existed beyond the contrived efforts of Eugénie. At the most fundamental level, both women were mistrusted by various circles as foreigners and were given similar snide epithets – Marie Antoinette as "the

Austrian woman" and Eugénie as "the Spanish woman." Both women also had the misfortune of inspiring general dislike among those whose support they desperately needed – namely, their husbands' families and the public. Of Eugénie, David Stacton wrote: "The family hated her and the French people did not love her very much. The family would have hated anybody, but for the opinion of France she herself was largely to blame."

Part of the problem may have been that Eugénie – like Marie Antoinette before her – frequently railed and rebelled against rigid Court etiquette. In her late 19th century book, "France in the Nineteenth Century," Elizabeth Wormeley Latimer wrote: "Brought up in private life, not early trained to the self-abnegation demanded of princesses, the Empress Eugénie did not bring into her new sphere all the *aplomb* and seriousness about little things which are early inculcated on ladies brought up to the profession of royalty." She continued: "With the impetuosity of her disposition and the intrepidity that had characterized her girlhood, she found it hard to submit to the restraints of her position, and the emperor had occasion frequently to remonstrate with her on her indifference to etiquette and public opinion."

The relationship Eugénie shared with her husband also echoed in some ways that of Marie Antoinette and Louis XVI. Both women had strong personalities and ultimately dominated their husbands' weaker natures – a circumstance that eventually helped bring about the downfall of both royal couples. In the end, like her icon, Eugénie became a scapegoat for the disasters that befell her husband's reign. Certain that the disastrous Franco-Prussian War that ended the Second Empire had been of Eugénie's making, Napoleon III's cousin, Princess Mathilde, pronounced: "She and she alone has been the cause of all

France's misfortune." Such sentiments were shared by many, but most modern historians agree that Napoleon III was equally culpable, just as Louis XVI had been.

Fortunately for Eugénie, she managed to avoid the tragic fate of Marie Antoinette – if only just. When Napoleon III was forced to surrender during the Franco-Prussian War, the tide of public opinion turned sharply against Eugénie, who was acting as Regent. Trapped in the Tuileries, which was surrounded by angry mobs, she managed to escape the palace in disguise and go into exile in England. It's impossible not to wonder if Eugénie regretted her choice of idol during her time of crisis. Did the idea of sharing Marie Antoinette's fate cause her to see her emulation as folly, even momentarily? Or did it have the opposite effect of further inspiring her to survive, not just in the name of self-preservation, but also as the "reincarnation" of Marie Antoinette?

We can never know the answers to these questions, but at the dramatic end of her reign and in so many other moments of tragedy, Eugénie had the personal wherewithal to display the same characteristics that even today inspire the most respect for Marie Antoinette – courage and dignity in her fate.

An Unusual Journey Through Royal History

Princess Ka'iulani: Princess of the Peacocks

It's not often you run across a Victorian-era princess with a surfboard named after her, never mind a Victorian-era princess who actually surfed, but Princess Ka'iulani of Hawaii was just such a rarity. And while it's refreshing to think of historical royalty in this light, surfing is the least of the characteristics that made Ka'iulani such a unique and important royal figure in her own time, not to mention today.

Born Princess Victoria Kawekiu Lunalilo Kalaninuiahilapalapa Ka'iulani Cleghorn on October 16, 1875 in Honolulu, Hawaii, her name reflected both her royal heritage - Ka'iulani translates to "royal sacred one" or "the highest point in heaven" - and Hawaii's political ties to Great Britain - Queen Victoria had been friendly to Hawaii's royalty. As for her surname, in case you hadn't already suspected, it reflected her non-royal heritage - that of her Scottish father, Archibald Cleghorn, a successful local businessman who was born in Edinburgh and emigrated to Hawaii as a young man.

In 1870, the 35-year-old Cleghorn married 19-year-old Miriam Likelike, who was from a family of important Hawaiian chiefs. Just four years later, her brother was elected King of Hawaii after his predecessor died without a successor, and Likelike became a royal princess. After the birth of Princess Ka'iulani the following year, the family seemed to live a pleasant existence at Ainahau, their estate in Waikiki, until the untimely death of Princess Likelike in 1887.

If there had previously been any doubt that Ka'iulani might someday inherit the Hawaiian throne, it vanished with her mother's death. Both the reigning monarch, King Kalākaua, and his heir, Princess Lili'uokalani - Ka'iulani's uncle and aunt, respectively - were childless, making Ka'iulani second in line to the throne. Accordingly, her father and royal relatives intended that the young Princess should receive an education befitting a future queen, and that included sending the young Princess to Britain. But not before she could earn some important admirers in her homeland.

Just five months before leaving Hawaii in May of 1889, Ka'iulani would meet and become fast friends with Robert Louis Stevenson, who was so impressed with the 13-year-old Princess - and she with him - that their short relationship is something of a legend. In honor of her departure for Britain, her wrote a poem for the Princess that includes the touching lines:

"Light of heart and bright of face:
The daughter of a double race.
Her islands here, in Southern sun, Shall mourn their Kaiulani gone..."

The two would never meet again - Stevenson died in 1894 on the Island of Samoa while Ka'iulani was in Britain, but Stevenson's words would eventually come to symbolize far more than Ka'iulani's temporary departure from Hawaii in 1889.

But first, she would be trained and primed for her future role as Queen of Hawaii - one that inched even closer when her uncle, King Kalākaua, died in January of 1891, leaving her aunt as the new monarch. Queen Lili'uokalani quickly cemented Ka'iulani's position by formally naming her as her heir. It would seem logical that, at this point, the new Crown Princess would have returned to Hawaii. After all, it was originally planned that her studies in Britain would last only one year and by the time of her elevation to Crown Princess, she had been studying to great success for more than two years, but all was not well in Hawaii.

When Queen Lili'uokalani attempted to strengthen the power of the monarchy soon after her accession, Americans in Hawaii who were afraid of losing their profitable sugar-cane interests led an uprising that eventually led to the Queen being deposed in 1893. Ka'iulani learned of the fall of her family from the throne while she was in Britain. Despite her heartbreak, the 17-year-old traveled to the United States to publicly fight that country's abolition of the Hawaiian monarchy and planned annexation of Hawaii.

Despite initial mocking by the U.S. press, who called her - among other things - the "heathen Princess," Ka'iulani won them over and was soon being described as "charming, fascinating" and "the very flower - an exotic - of civilization." More importantly, she won over President Grover Cleveland, who promised to help her cause, although his efforts were ineffectual.

Ka'iulani returned to Britain - where, in 1894, she learned that Hawaii had become a republic - and, eventually, elsewhere in Europe, before finally returning to Hawaii in 1897. Since learning of the fall of the monarchy, Ka'iulani's health had deteriorated to the point of chronic migraine headaches and easy susceptibility to other ailments. After years of living in the cooler climates of Britain, her health only became worse in the warm, tropical weather of her homeland. Despite her health, Ka'iulani continued to live at Ainahau, enjoying her passions of riding, horticulture and, of course, the many beloved peacocks that lived on her estate - a passion that earned her one of her many favorable nicknames, "The Princess of the Peacocks." Her people admired her and she continued to be an important figure in her homeland.

But all that would end abruptly in 1898 when she caught a fever after riding one day in the rain. Her health never improved and she died on March 6, 1899, at only 23 years of age. In her wake, schools, hotels and, yes, even surfboards, have been named for her and she continues to be a representative of all that was - and still is - good about Hawaii.

BORN TO RULE, LIKE IT OR NOT

Chances are, at one time or another, you've hated your job and have reveled in the idea – if not the deed itself – of making a proud and elaborate show of ending your misery by flat out quitting, preferably after using a few choice words in final retaliation. Whether you hated your boss, were unhappy with your salary, disliked your working conditions, or just realized that you were in the wrong profession, it's unlikely that you were ever lacking choice in the matter – either stay and tough it out or quit and find something more appealing or fulfilling. And, whether you like your job or not, you live in full expectation of someday retiring and living out your golden years any way you choose.

While there are many aspects of royal life that we can envy, this ability to choose our path in life is one of the clear advantages of being a commoner. Unlike a sovereign or an heir to the throne, you were not born into a role that you are expected to fulfill for your entire life without question or hesitation. Not that the choices of those born to fill a throne aren't simple – they can reign and die or reign and abdicate. Many have chosen the latter option and, as a result, they frequently live on in the public consciousness more so than their counterparts who chose the former option.

Of course, the first abdication that comes to mind for most people today is that of Britain's King Edward VIII. But abdication is as old as monarchy itself and has never discriminated against race, sex or nationality. Whether forced or voluntary, Roman emperors, kings and queens, hereditary princes and grand dukes and, yes, even popes have abdicated. In times past, the primary impetus for abdication was frequently either political and/or popular upheaval or military loss, although both were undoubtedly the cause of abdications well into the 20th century. In fact, no fewer than 44 European monarchs (including princes and grand dukes) either abdicated or were deposed between World Wars I and II.

In more modern times, where monarchs tend to reign rather than rule, abdication frequently has more to do with personal interests that outweigh the monarch's desire to do the job – as was the case with Edward VIII – or, increasingly, a desire to "pass the torch," so to speak, to the younger generation. And while personal choice is almost certainly a modern invention, even where royalty is concerned, the idea of abdication as retirement is actually not a new one. Between the years 1555 and 1556, 55-year-old Holy Roman Emperor Charles V abdicated as ruler of each of his various domains – including Spain, the Netherlands, Austria and Germany – in order to retire to a monastery in Spain and tend to his gout. Many modern monarchs have done the same and, especially where age and/or ill health are factors, it's perhaps the most understandable of all forms of abdication.

One of the most recent modern abdications falls to Norodom Sihanouk, who abdicated his position as King of Cambodia on October 7, 2004, citing poor health, and is now grandly known as "The Great Heroic King Sihanouk." Other monarchies have turned "retirement" abdication into something of a family tradition. In the Netherlands, Queen Wilhelmina couldn't possibly have realized that her voluntary abdication on September 4, 1948 would start a trend in her family. After more than 50 years as Queen of the Netherlands, she simply wanted to retire. As it turned out, her successor – her daughter Juliana – would do the same more than 30 years later in favor of her own daughter, the reigning Queen Beatrix. Interestingly, Wilhelmina is said to have considered abdicating more than once during the 1930s, a period when she felt unable to work with the government to reverse the economic depression of her country. According to Geoffrey Hindley in his book *The Royal Families of Europe*, "Wilhelmina's great grandfather William I had abdicated because the newly emergent state of Belgium marked the failure of his policies. For Wilhelmina, abdication seemed the only tolerable perhaps honourable solution to her frustrated desire to help her country."

Another family that has made abdication as retirement something of a tradition is Luxembourg, although the family's first abdication wasn't quite so positive. When Grand Duchess Marie-Adélaïde inherited the throne on her father's death in 1912, she considered herself sovereign by the grace of God and became politically controversial enough that, by 1919, the government demanded her abdication. She was succeeded by her sister, Charlotte, who reigned as Grand Duchess until she made a far more positive abdication on November 12, 1964, in favor of her eldest son, Jean. The new reigning Grand Duke had actually been Grand Duchess Charlotte's Lieutenant-Representative (essentially a Regent) for three years prior to her abdication – a period that was undoubtedly meant to give her son time to acclimate to his future role under her guidance. The concept worked well enough that Grand Duke Jean followed his mother's lead and, in 1998, made his own son, Henri,

Lieutenant-Representative, before abdicating the throne altogether on October 7, 2000. Although it remains to be seen, it's not beyond reason to suspect that reigning Grand Duke Henri will eventually do the same with his son, Prince Guillame.

Naturally, there is the rare instance of a monarch using abdication as a temporary political or personal device. This was certainly the case when, in 1990, King Baudouin of Belgium, a deeply religious man, was faced with giving Royal Assent to legislation that liberalized Belgium's abortion laws. Unwilling to give his official endorsement to what he found personally objectionable, the King chose instead to temporarily abdicate his throne on April 4th, the day he was expected to sign the bill. He was back to work the following day and continued to reign until his death in 1993.

By now you may have noticed that none of the positive examples of abdication are related to Britain. Clearly, while a great many cases of abdication on the Continent have been negative, it seems that Britain's association with abdication is a terminally negative one. Although some will point to Edward VIII's abdication in 1936 as the main reason that abdication is such a dirty word in Britain, Geoffrey Hindley draws another conclusion, again in *The Royal Families of Europe*, "Among European royal houses abdication does not have the negative resonances associated with it in the English tradition. Here it has been a ten-letter work of blackest omen ever since in 1399 Richard II made the 'voluntary gesture' of resignation to his cousin Henry IV and was never seen alive again." An excellent point considering that Richard II's abdication was, in fact, a forced deposition, not unlike that of Scotland's Queen Mary and Britain's James II. In fact, I'm at a loss to cite one single abdication in British history that has been a "good" one.

An Unusual Journey Through Royal History

As if the connotation of abdication wasn't already bad enough in Britain – what with all those monarchs being forced to abdicate and another voluntarily abdicating for a so-called "horrid" American woman – the reputation of the act can be further associated with Georgian-era monarchs behaving more like spoiled children determined to get their way. Two cases in point – George III and George IV. In 1783, with Tory Prime Minister Shelbourne's government in ruin, George III was appalled at the idea of accepting a Whig as prime minister. As his desperate bid to convince any Tory politician of merit to start a government began to crumble before him, he began drafting his abdication speech and even considered leaving England instead of accept a Whig. He eventually came to his senses and, resuming his dignity, accepted Whig politician Charles James Fox as the new prime minister. Like father, like son – shortly after his ascension to the throne, George IV threatened to abdicate rather than accept his wife Caroline as queen consort. Instead, Queen Caroline literally had the door unceremoniously slammed in her face when she attempted to attend her husband's coronation. Luckily for the future of the new king's reign, Caroline died shortly thereafter.

Of course, there is at least one aspect of abdication that ties all monarchies together and that is monarchs who just weren't fit to rule. Although it has never been officially considered as a pretext to abdication, suitability for the job has certainly come into question on more than one occasion in every monarchy. While physical and mental defects play a big role in unsuitability, more than a few such monarchs have lived out their reign with one or both conditions, generally with the help of a regent. Surprisingly, it is personal faults that have had a more disastrous effect because, although it's possible to train an individual for the job they were born to take, a personality or temperament cannot always be so easily molded. To make matters worse, it has frequently occurred that an individual is not only unsuited to the job, but also untrained, as in the case of a second son who was not initially expected to take on the role of monarch.

It almost goes without saying that a great many monarchs in history were not only ill-equipped to effectively carry out their role (many to their own admission), but were also drastic liabilities to their domains. Among these individuals, the lucky ones managed either to live out their reign or were forced to abdicate, while the unlucky met with overthrow and execution. At least if you do badly in your job, the worst you'll get is fired.

THE ROYAL NUNNERY

It's no secret that George III's sons were notoriously naughty, with the Prince of Wales leading the pack. "Prinny," as the future George IV was known, committed every transgression he possibly could and then some. No need to beat a dead horse there. The younger sons put every ounce of their energy into keeping up with big brother, and didn't do a half bad job. With little real control over his sons, the king could only watch, grow frustrated, and occasionally make various weak threats.

But his daughters were a different matter altogether. They could be controlled.

Like the witch to Rapunzel, George III locked his daughters away from the world at large, hoping against hope to keep them pure and untouched. Far from carrying on the tradition of grooming royal princesses to live as foreign consorts and royal breeding machines, the six princesses – Charlotte, Augusta, Elizabeth, Mary, Sophia and Amelia – were trained to be lifelong spinsters and helpmeets to their parents.

Although the king was said to have been a doting and loving father, he was possessive and controlling with both his wife and his daughters, wishing them to be devoted to him alone and doing his best to eliminate outside influences and court intrigues from their lives. To this end, he demanded that the princesses be raised in a strict and isolated environment designed to allow them little contact with the outside world and, in particular, to keep them as far away from men as possible.

George's wife, Queen Charlotte, had come to her husband as a young and inexperienced German princess, and was almost immediately detached from normal court life under his controlling influences. Secluded and lonely, she subjugated herself to her husband in nearly everything and became, according to most reports, a bitter and defensive woman. Unfortunately for her daughters, Charlotte was largely responsible for their upbringing and, under the king's direction, ensured that their lives were as lonely, suffocating and isolated as her own.

Under the best of circumstances, the young princesses could read nothing that hadn't been approved, were rarely without a chaperone, and had every hour of their day planned for them. Although not entirely unusual for young women of the upper classes, these traditions were taken to the extreme with the royal princesses. Even as adults, their parents outlined the princesses' daily lives, allowing few opportunities for deviation.

Among the most oppressive conditions, the princesses were forced to attend their mother by standing behind her chair for hours at a time, sometimes falling asleep on their feet. They were also required not to speak to the king unless spoken to and to stand when engaging in a conversation with him. Like the king's courtiers, the princesses had to leave a room walking backward in the king's presence.

Despite the restrictions, they were exposed under controlled conditions to the arts and other acceptable pastimes and were considered accomplished young women. Under the tutelage of masters like Thomas Gainsborough, Charlotte and Elizabeth became talented amateur artists. Augusta and Amelia were music lovers, and Sophia a skilled horsewoman. But while such skills and talents were generally nurtured in young women to attract good husbands, this was not the case for the princesses. Since the king didn't want his daughters to marry, eligible men of the princesses' age were not allowed into their circle and suitable matches with members of foreign royalty were rarely entertained. With access only to their father, brothers and, occasionally, household staff, the girls knew little of the opposite sex.

The princesses referred to their cloistered existence as "the nunnery."

Under these circumstances, it would seem logical that the girls would have had little opportunity to stray from the path of chaste and obedient royal princesses. On the other hand, sheltered as they were from even the more virtuous pleasures of the Georgian age, it is perhaps more understandable that they took the opposite course by settling for existences considered either unpleasant or unsuitable even to their lower class contemporaries.

In desperate attempts to escape the nunnery, three of the princesses took their chances at late marriages to men who were, on the whole, repellant. The first to embark on this path was Charlotte, the Princess Royal, who – though not ugly by any stretch of the imagination – was widely considered to be the least beautiful of all the daughters. In 1797, at the age of 30 she married the extremely fat King Frederick of Württemberg, whose first wife had died under mysterious circumstances while she was imprisoned under his orders. Nevertheless, Charlotte was considered lucky to escape the nunnery.

The next to marry was Mary who, at 40, wed her first cousin, the Duke of Gloucester, better known as "Silly Billy" and considered to be something of a tyrant. Third and last to marry was Elizabeth, who became the 48-year-old bride of Frederick VI of Hesse-Homburg, whose hygiene habits were reportedly appalling (it's said that he almost never bathed). Perhaps not surprisingly (age or revulsion, take your pick), the marriages produced no living children. Only Charlotte, who married the youngest, had a child – a stillborn daughter.

It's actually a wonder that these three managed to secure permission at all for their marriages, but it's not unlikely that they took advantage of their father's many bouts with illness. The remaining three princesses were not so "lucky." They were doomed to fall for men who were entirely unsuitable as the husband of a princess and had no chance of gaining George III's approval, no matter what his mental or physical state. With the limited number of men at the princesses' disposal, it is no coincidence that each of them fell in love with their father's equerries, perhaps the first and only outside men to come into their lives.

Augusta, who had early on been considered as a potential bride for the Crown Prince of Denmark, fell in love with Sir Brent Spencer, one of her father's equerries. She showed a great deal of spirit on behalf of her cause, going as far as pleading with her brother, who was then Prince Regent, to allow her to marry Spencer. Although there is some speculation that a private marriage may actually have taken place, it is historically unfounded and highly unlikely. Augusta died, unmarried, at the age of 72, early in Queen Victoria's reign.

The baby of the family, Amelia was even less lucky, certainly in love, but also in health. Around the age of 17, she fell in love with yet another of George IIIs equerries, Sir Charles FitzRoy, who was said to be a very dull young man. Because she was under 25, Amelia knew she could not marry FitzRoy without the king's consent, which she would never receive. Instead, she held out hope that, after her 25th birthday, she could request permission from Parliament. Illness and other factors prevented this, but while she never actually married FitzRoy, she *considered* herself married to him and signed her correspondence with the initials "AFR", for Amelia FitzRoy. She was not to enjoy her fantasy for long. Always a sickly child, she was chronically ill after 1795 and died of tuberculosis in 1810 at the age of 27.

Of all the daughters, Sophia – considered the most clever and one of the most attractive – made the greatest, and perhaps most shocking, departure from her upbringing. Always unhealthy, Sophia is now considered to have shared a form of her father's illness, porphyria (the disease that we now understand to have been the cause of his so-called "madness"). As a result of the family's combined health problems, Sophia and her sisters made frequent visits to the southern coastal town of Weymouth for resting and cures.

Another of George III's equerries, General Thomas Garth, leased a house not far from Weymouth in order to be near the king during his visits. Sophia and her sisters would stop at this house on their journey to Weymouth, and it was here that Sophia was said to have an affair with General Garth. As unlikely a candidate as there ever was, Garth was 56-years-old, very short, and had a large, disfiguring purple birthmark covering his face.

Nevertheless, in August 1800, at the age of 22, Sophia gave birth to a boy she named Thomas, undoubtedly after his father. Apparently, the entire family – save the king – knew of Sophia's pregnancy and the subsequent birth of her son. To explain

Sophia's increasing size and necessary absence away from the family, the king was told that she was bloated due to dropsy and had to be sent away to recover. Upon her return to court, the king was informed she had been given a miraculous cure consisting of roast beef, which brought about an immediate recovery. The king was suspicious, but accepted the story.

The newborn child was left at the Weymouth home of the king's private secretary, Colonel Herbert Taylor, then later adopted by General Garth himself. While the palace never officially recognized the existence of Thomas, the unofficial stance was that General Garth was indeed the natural father and this was generally accepted at court. It didn't stop a nasty rumor from circulating, however, claiming that Sophia's brother Ernest, Duke of Cumberland, had incestuously raped her and was the "real" father of the child.

In any case, General Garth retained his position at court and was even appointed to the household of the Prince of Wales' daughter, Princess Charlotte. Sophia returned to her life as before and, after the death of her parents, lived a spinster in Kensington Palace until she died in 1848 at the age of 71. Her son, the younger Thomas Garth died in 1839.

While it might be easy to pin King George III's extreme behavior on his so-called "madness," it's quite possible that he was, in fact, reacting to the tragic lives of his sisters, for which he was partially responsible. Things might have turned out differently if George's father, Frederick, Prince of Wales, hadn't died prematurely in 1751. The 13-year-old George, his four brothers and four sisters, were left in the care of the Dowager Princess of Wales until 1760, when, at the age of 22, George succeeded his grandfather, King George II, and became head of the family.

One sister, Elizabeth Caroline – who one contemporary described as a "dwarf" – had died the year before at the tender age of 18 of inflammation of the bowels. She and her younger sister Louisa Anne had both suffered from ill health virtually from birth. Elizabeth could not stand without assistance, and had been so unhealthy as a child that she hadn't been taught to read. The two invalid sisters were close companions and, after Elizabeth's death, Louisa's health rapidly deteriorated.

There is a touching portrait of Louisa, age six, by Jean-Étienne Liotard in the Royal Collection that beautifully exposes her youth and fragility. As was the custom at that time, she is pictured wearing the same type of formal gown worn by grown women, only in miniature. The cut of the gown exposes her chest, giving her the look of a little girl playing "dress-up." Sadly, she was truly as fragile as her portrait suggested and she died of tuberculosis when she was 19.

Ill health may have taken the lives of Elizabeth and Louisa before they were out of their teens, but it saved them from the disastrous marriages that made the lives of their healthier sisters miserable. In 1764, in a purely political move, George arranged the marriage of his elder sister Augusta to Charles II, Duke of Brunswick. The marriage was extremely unhappy, the Duke was said to be "coarse and brutal," and Augusta hated Germany. The couple's three sons were defective in health and intellect, while their daughter, Caroline of Brunswick, married George III's own son, The Prince of Wales (the future George IV) – a notoriously bad match.

With Augusta's marriage and departure to her new home in Germany, only the ailing Louisa and the King's youngest sister, Caroline Matilda, remained to be dealt with. In fact, Caroline's fate had already been determined a year before

Augusta's marriage. King Frederick V of Denmark had come calling at George III's court, seeking a wife for his eldest son Christian. Frederick's first wife – and Christian's mother – had been George III's aunt, another Princess Louisa. Coincidentally, the sickly Louisa Anne was originally chosen as Christian's future wife, but Frederick's envoy decided that the healthier and attractive Caroline Matilda was a better candidate.

Her health and good looks may have secured her marriage to the heir to the Danish throne, but they would not secure her happiness. Caroline Matilda's tragic story cannot be done justice in such a short space, but the abbreviated version goes something like this...

The marriage was arranged in 1763, but since the princess was only 12, it was decided that the wedding would wait until she was at least 15, and the engagement was not announced until January 1765. Although King George had reservations about his sister marrying and being sent to a foreign country so young, he was under pressure to make what was viewed as a politically advantageous match, and he agreed that the marriage would take place within two years. Almost exactly one year after the announcement of the engagement, King Frederick V's death further accelerated the wedding plans, and on October 1, 1766, 15-year-old Caroline Matilda was married by proxy to 18-year-old King Christian VII of Denmark.

The following day, she left her family and home for Denmark. Prohibited from bringing her attendants from home, she was surrounded by unfamiliar people in a strange land, without even the benefit of speaking their language. To make matters worse, she quickly discovered that her new husband was not quite right. Deformed and schizophrenic, his behavior was erratic at best and outrageous at worst. Despite what was certainly an extremely unhappy existence, Caroline managed to bear Christian a son and heir in 1768, the future King Frederick VI.

By 1769, she had become extremely ill and was eventually put under the care of the royal physician, Johann Friedrich Struensée. The two soon began having an affair, which Caroline did little to hide. As the love affair between the queen and the doctor grew, so Christian's mental capacity deteriorated, and the pair was soon effectively running the government in the king's place. When she gave birth to a daughter in 1771, Struensée was widely believed to be the father, and powers in the court began to conspire against the queen and her lover.

In 1772, Christian's stepmother forced him to sign a document ordering the arrest of Struensée and the 20-year-old queen. Both parties confessed to the affair and Struensée was tortured and executed, while Caroline – as the sister of George III – was spared. She was divorced from Christian, separated from her children, and sent to live in exile in Celle, Hanover. She died there, aged 23, in 1775.

At the time of Caroline Matilda's arrest in Denmark, George III's eldest daughter, Princess Charlotte, was just 5 years old, and his need to control his family was ever increasing. Two of his brothers were actually the impetus for the introduction of the 1772 Royal Marriages Act, which prohibits any descendant of George II to marry under the age of 25 without the monarch's permission. Many of the relationship troubles of royalty over the last 230 years can be effectively blamed on George III's scandal-prone brother Henry, Duke of Cumberland, who secretly married the commoner and widow, Anne Horton, in 1771. Almost immediately after the Act was passed, the king's favorite brother, William, Duke of Gloucester, admitted that he, too, had secretly married a widowed commoner, Lady Waldegrave, in 1766.

Shattered over the unfortunate and unhappy events of his sister's lives and unable to control the behavior of his brothers and, later, his sons, perhaps the king was simply overcompensating where his daughters were concerned. As a loving but misguided father who already leaned toward over protectiveness and extreme behavior, it is not difficult to see how circumstances could have affected and enhanced his controlling behavior toward his daughters. Unfortunately, his was a self-fulfilling prophecy – instead of protecting his daughters, he led them into fates not far removed from those of his sisters.

Queen Kleptomaniac?

Queen Mary probably did more to perpetuate the image of a queen as a stately, heavily bejeweled, dignified and distant figure than any other English queen before or since. At her best, she was acutely aware of her royal heritage, always conscious of her position and, most importantly, devoted to duty above all else. At her worst, she showed little passion or emotion for anything in life other than "duty," including her children, with the exception of collecting.

Although she started collecting with a vengeance upon her accession, World War I put a temporary stop to her efforts and it wasn't until after the war that she began spending much of her free time collecting, redecorating, restoring, and even making personal trips to antique shops, where she would seek out porcelain, paintings, or items with a royal connection of some kind.

Her favorite collectibles included jeweled fans, jewels, and *objets d'art*, although her overall collection included everything from royal seals to cameos to Fabergé animals to gold boxes encrusted with jewels. Later in life, she kept no fewer than 90 valuable objects at the writing table in her private sitting room.

Although she seemed to follow a Victorian love of amassing and displaying lots of "things," her collecting had at least one strong cohesive theme: the royal family. Hugo Vickers wrote to me: "It is worth noting that she admired a bad portrait of a family relation much higher than a really important work of art with no royal connection!" James Pope-Hennessy, in his biography of Queen Mary, talks at length of her obsessive zeal for "reorganizing the Royal collections and the furniture in the Royal residences, and of retrieving portraits, plate, pieces of furniture, miniatures and relics which had, in earlier years, been dispersed and which she now re-integrated into the collections at Windsor Castle" (not to mention Buckingham Palace, Balmoral and Holyrood House). Similarly, according to Leslie Field, Queen Mary's careful planning made the royal family's jewel collection what it is today.

But it was her method of obtaining objects for her collections that raises eyebrows. Even today, she is widely known to have "politely" connived the owners of valuable objects she desired to either give her the objects as gifts or sell them to her at ridiculously low prices. In "Royal Babylon," Karl Shaw claims that she even surreptitiously pocketed items that would later be returned to the owners by her aides. Famously, when gazing upon an object of desire, she would announce, "I am caressing it with my eyes." Or, just before leaving the residence containing the item she longed to obtain, she would ask, "May I go back and say goodbye to that dear little _____?"

But these were small-scale operations, so to speak. Queen Mary, it seems, was no novice, and more than once she got away with something akin to the crown jewels. In particular, her notorious acquisition of the Romanov jewels is threaded with scandal.

When Russia's Dowager Empress Marie Feodorovna, sister of England's Queen Alexandra, escaped the Russian Revolution, she brought with her the remains of one of the most magnificent jewelry collections history had ever seen. After her death, her remaining two daughters wished to sell the jewels to provide an income for themselves, so turned to their cousin, King George V for help. But, according to author Suzy Menkes, Queen Mary took advantage of the king's sudden illness and underhandedly selected for herself several pieces in the collection, offering to pay only half the valuation price. As it turned out, she didn't even pay the amount she offered, a debt that was later honored by Queen Elizabeth to the descendents of the grand duchesses Queen Mary had cheated.

There is also the slightly less dubious incident where Queen Mary had to finagle the Cambridge emeralds from her late brother's mistress. These emeralds, now in the Queen's collection, were won in a lottery in the early 1800's and were passed down from Augusta of Cambridge to Queen Mary's mother, eventually making their way into the hands of Queen Mary's brother, Prince Frank. Although his contemporaries stated that the emeralds had been bequeathed specifically to him and would therefore have been his to do with as he wished, a family incident ensued after his death where it is said Queen Mary successfully bribed her brother's mistress to return the jewels.

Of course, she also managed to get her hands on some of the most important diamonds of her time and, in particular, what was to become the most valuable brooch in the world. The Cullinan diamond, all 3025 carats of it, had been cut into the two enormous stones now set in the Crown Jewels, as well as more than 100 additional smaller stones. While the two main stones were considered to belong to the Crown, rather than any individual, the remaining stones were purchased privately and, in 1910, the High Commissioner of South Africa presented

Queen Mary with 102 of them, which are still known today in the royal family as "Granny's chips."

The two largest of these diamonds, the 92-carat pear shaped Cullinan III and 62-carat square cut Cullinan IV, were set into one extremely large brooch. This amazing piece of jewelry, along with all the other stones that were set into various other amazing pieces of jewelry were Queen Mary's private property. Quite a trick considering they were originally meant for the Crown. Even Queen Elizabeth inherited these items as personal property, although the brooch has now made its way back to being Crown property.

But whether it was pocketing valuable *objets d'art* from stately homes or the dubious acquisition of priceless jewels, Queen Mary's "collecting" went beyond the norm. It's been said that a deprived childhood can lead to obsessive collecting as an adult. In relative terms, Queen Mary had just such a childhood, growing up as something of a poor royal relation whose parents were riddled with money problems, so perhaps her amassing of valuable objects as queen was compensation.

There is at least one occasion in her life where she seems to have been acting out such a scenario. As a child, she had traveled widely to the royal courts of her wealthier relations where she had been made to feel inferior and unimportant. She had her revenge in 1913 when, as Queen Consort of England, she literally covered herself head to toe with diamonds to attend the wedding of Kaiser Wilhelm's daughter. To her great satisfaction, she was widely hailed as being the most spectacular individual at the gathering.

On the other hand, perhaps her actions were more clinical than psychological. Queen Mary could perhaps have suffered from kleptomania, which science now indicates may be the result of a chemical imbalance in the brain. This in no way implies that she was practicing a royal form of shoplifting, as the disease is defined as the failure to resist the impulse to steal items that are not needed for personal use or monetary value. And Queen Mary certainly did not need the money.

So was it obsessive collecting or kleptomania? Deprived childhood or lack of the chemical serotonin? As with many of the so-called "darker" aspects of royal history, we're unlikely to know for certain. But perhaps the answer can be derived from Queen Mary herself, who claimed that she got her love of collecting from her father, although, she clarified, "he was poor and could not afford to buy." In the end, maybe she was simply on a single-minded mission to retrieve something in life that she felt her father had missed and, in the process, restore his dignity as well as her own. Or maybe not.

More Books by Victoria Martínez

"The Royal W.E. Unique Glimpses of The Duke and Duchess of Windsor" eBook only http://whodareswinspublishing.com

Most people think they know the story of King Edward VIII giving up his throne for the woman he loved, Wallis Simpson, in 1936. The truth is: politics and innuendo clouded that story from the very beginning, with the result that few people really understand who The Duke and Duchess of Windsor were and what forces propelled them to their infamous fate.

The Royal W.E. examines the individual and intertwined lives of Wallis and Edward – or "W.E." as they referred to themselves – and provides readers with unique glimpses of the real people, as opposed to the sensationalized characters, that were The Duke and Duchess of Windsor.

Through careful study of more than 75 years of rhetoric and scholarship, Victoria Martínez takes on the most controversial charges lodged against the couple (Was Wallis a hermaphrodite? Were the Duke and Duchess Nazi sympathizers?) with candor and evenhandedness. In analyzing the early lives of Wallis and the ex-king and their later relationships with other members of the Royal Family, her approach is to deal with all parties as human beings, whose true faults – though significant – were far less sinister than history has led us to believe. Ms. Martínez also addresses the ever-popular subject of the Duchess's jewels, including new research on the famous 1946 Ednam Lodge jewel heist to dispel the long-held rumors that the Duke and Duchess committed jewel theft and insurance fraud.

The subjects in this book are not always mainstream, well known, or even consistent with "popular" opinion, and the objective is not to make anyone "like" the couple. Instead, readers will find refreshingly honest and accurate portrayals of W.E. that will help them understand the real people behind the myth and hype.

"Prejudice and preconception are difficult things to set aside, particularly after so many years of negative stories and sordid rumor, but I think readers here will discover an alternative and convincing look at the Duke and Duchess of Windsor. I am sure *they* would approve and perhaps, just perhaps, the future may be a little bit kinder to Edward and Wallis because of the efforts of people like Ms. Martínez." -Greg King, author of *The Duchess of Windsor: The Uncommon Life of Wallis Simpson*

AUTHOR BIO

Victoria (Tori) V. Martínez researches and writes about history, both from her current home in Texas and on her frequent trips abroad with her husband David. Tori, an American, likes to joke that she only married David, a Spaniard she met in England, because his knowledge of seven languages helps her immensely in her historical research.

Tori works as a freelance public relations professional, which allows her to travel, research and write. She earned her undergraduate degree in Mass Communications from Texas Woman's University and her graduate degree in Applied Technology, Training and Development from The University of North Texas. After working in the corporate world for several years, Tori realized her passion for writing about history was what made her happy, so she packed up her life in America and spent two years living abroad.

Although fate currently has her living back in the U.S., she spends as much time as possible writing, researching and traveling. Her historical writing has been published online at sites like the Unofficial Royalty website (http://www.unofficialroyalty.com) and TimeTravel-Britain.com, and in print journals such as *The European Royal History Journal, Royalty Digest Quarterly* and *The Duke and Duchess of Windsor Society Quarterly*. She also served as a historical consultant for the BBC Radio 4 Saturday Play, "The Windsor Jewels," a subject she has written about extensively.

"An Unusual Journey Through Royal History, Volume I" was her first book and was published in April 2011. Her second book, "The Royal W.E. Unique Glimpses of The Duke and Duchess of Windsor," was published in June 2011. A combined print book of both volumes of "An Unusual Journey Through Royal History" is due to be published in January 2012.

Tori can be found at her personal website, http://www.victoriahill.com, and her Arbitrary History Blog at http://www.arbitraryhistory.com.

Victoria Martínez

An Unusual Journey Through Royal History

Victoria Martínez

CPSIA information can be obtained at www.ICGtesting.com
Printed in the USA
LVOW040912140212

268590LV00001B/3/P